TALES
from the
ORCHARD

H.B. WEST

outskirts
press

Tales from the Orchard
All Rights Reserved.
Copyright © 2020 H.B. West
v1.0

The opinions expressed in this manuscript are solely the opinions of the author and do not represent the opinions or thoughts of the publisher. The author has represented and warranted full ownership and/or legal right to publish all the materials in this book.

This book may not be reproduced, transmitted, or stored in whole or in part by any means, including graphic, electronic, or mechanical without the express written consent of the publisher except in the case of brief quotations embodied in critical articles and reviews.

Outskirts Press, Inc.
http://www.outskirtspress.com

ISBN: 978-1-9772-2472-9

Cover Photo © 2020 H.B. West. All rights reserved - used with permission.

Outskirts Press and the "OP" logo are trademarks belonging to Outskirts Press, Inc.

PRINTED IN THE UNITED STATES OF AMERICA

Foreword
[Tales from the Orchard]

I first met H. Barton West on a fly fishing trip to the Salmon River in New York. I don't remember catching any fish. After two days I was sure Bart and I had been friends for all of our sixty-plus years. We became fishing, hunting, storytelling, and Tennessee sour mash sippin companions. At the time I didn't know he would become a favorite author. I should have.

Bart can tell a tale like few others. His love of all things outdoors (OK, a number of indoor things too, particularly if there is a friendly waitress) sure helps and comes through on every page but his words, sometimes sparse, make you want to be right there with him. Every now and then I have to stop to remember that Bart's tales are true. Oh, I wouldn't bet against a little polish having been applied here and there, but the adventures in *Tales from the Orchard* are vivid pictures of a full life. They are frequently humorous, sometimes educational, occasionally disjointed, but always leave you wanting more. Whether recounting fishing in Alaska or quail hunting in Georgia, Bart just naturally has the reader by his side - and very happily.

You will be comfortable in the Orchard and its environs - just as Bart is even if he may try not to admit it. Rural Maryland comes to life. Walking lonely fields with springer Jack in 2008 or following General Hancock and his troops along country roads in 1863, you will see it clearly. Friends Creek will enchant you. A more beautiful spot is hard to picture - Bart does it easily. Of course, there are the 'bows and browns. What a delightful person is the Orchard's Miss Grace. You'll be sure you can taste the lemonade and cookies at her for kids only Fox Hole Club. I guess there really are times when we wouldn't mind being ten again. Bart believes in tradition. He shares many of his. Bart and his great friend, J. R., move their TGIF tradition in Brewer's Alley in nearby Frederick up to Wednesday because Friday doesn't come early enough in the week, and they modify again when they "moved our charm, wit, and personalities, to say nothing of good looks" to the upscale Tasting Room. You will be absolutely charmed (can men use that word) to share Bart's tradition of Christmas with Kat at Friends Creek. Kat's violin, lunch on the deck with lobster bisque, cheese, a good wine:

> "The deck overlooks the Nutshell Pool from about fifteen feet above. Opened a pinot noir. The Pool was alive with rising trout, gulping, flashing, breaking the surface. Ravenous and aggressive, must have been a dozen or more, a hatch of some kind. High and fast water had submerged the Kilimanjaro rock. String up our rods, tie on a dry? Or drink our wine and just watch?"

What could be better, you have to read it yourself.

The Orchard is Bart's home. It has been for most of his seventy-plus years. He may spend considerable time in J.R.'s Georgia - it's the quail capital of the world and has plenty of 'bows and browns. He speaks frequently and fondly of Panama City Beach in Florida. Hopefully he will continue to go far and wide on memorable adventures. But he will always return to his 1840 home on main street. A Federal style red brick with a most inviting garden and rear deck just made for sippin as the sun sinks. You can walk all around the Orchard in half an hour, with time thrown in for "good mornings" to friendly neighbors. Bart writes there - too busy in the field except for brief notes. Bart dreams there - of his next rainbow in Alaska, a grouse or two in Maine, and maybe an Atlantic Salmon - anywhere. The added bonus is that we look forward to those tales in the second book.

I suspect you like outdoor stories and have your favorite writers, maybe just from the fact that you have picked up this book. Bart's writing will surprise you. Maybe a touch of Pinckney will peek through, but Bart's style is fresh and his own. You will laugh at, and with, Bart and his friends, maybe shed a tear, but mostly you will enjoy.

Brian E. Bennett
Front Royal, Virginia
April, 2019

DECEMBER 15, 2007
THE ORCHARD, MARYLAND

Almost ten months ago now I moved to The Orchard with my dog Jack. This is our first Christmas here. It's also our first Christmas alone.

I have deep roots here. This kitchen has traditionally been the gathering spot for generations of family, friends, neighbors and assorted reprobates.

I grew up in this kitchen. Despite the many fond memories of this place, I would rather be someplace else. Nowhere specific, I'd simply rather be anywhere else. I could not wait to leave here forty couple years ago and now I'm back here. Seems like a waste of those years.

Jack is happy here. He has his own door to a large fenced-in yard, which a variety of critters pass through from time to time. He does not realize we are stuck here. The necessary restoration to the house has left me cash poor. I realize we are stuck here. With that thought, I put another log on the fire and pour another round over the ice.

A blast of winter on the north wind rumbles in the chimney. The large fireplace built for cooking has cinnamon-flavored water simmering in the iron kettle. It's hissing, popping, and crackling as embers jump to the large red leather wing back chair. A flick of the wrist sends the hot embers to the brick floor. There is a tinkle of ice in an ample Irish crystal snifter covered over by Tennessee whiskey. It rests on a small table between the wingbacks. It was not the first one tonight. It complements the aroma from the kettle. It is a good time for philosophizing, wood fires, and good whiskey.

Jack is curled up on his dark green, round bed in front of the roaring fire, with flames well up the chimney. This is no small, cuddly, romantic fire. It is a blaze, fitting of two hunters' home from the hills. We had hunted pheasants in the afternoon. Jack and I flushed and retrieved four for the freezer. Jack is a joy to behold, smart, fast, biddable, yet he is a Springer. Not in his make-up to be perfect, just beautiful and fun to watch work. It is just the two of us this Christmas, as all my friends have families and were busy with their own plans. Tonight, Jack and I are tired, warm, and at peace with the world we have no need for company. Not that anyone would just stop by for a friendly whiskey, we are far too distant for that. The night is clear and cold. The whiskey tastes as it was meant to when accompanying a good cigar.

The memories that hang on the walls and by the fireplace have been with me all my life. My great-grandfather's Sharps musket hangs under the mantel. His Union cavalryman's sword is on the right sideboard. This is all that remain from his time. There are a dozen or so paintings, oils, and pastels on the wall as well. These bring back dim memories of my grandfather, but that is all from his time.

I have hung his still-life oil of fruit and a wine jug in the kitchen. The watermelon pastel is over the butler's sink. A Scottish Highlander's stag horn walking stick is hung to the left of the hearth. That stick not only is full of memories for me, it is also the inspiration to not be stuck, the spur to get me out of The Orchard and live life to the fullest of my ability.

I have never lived here without a dog. Jinx filled that role in my childhood. Jack does now.

My thoughts drift back to a slower time. Jinx and I hunting the springs and coverts of Cool Spring Farm, where the Union Army camped before heading to battle. I find myself wishing Jack and I could do the same tomorrow, but they are no more. Gone, to private property, no trespassing, no dogs, no guns.

Faintly, the wale of sirens disturbs my reminiscing, coming across Clear Ridge toward town. There was more than one. I gave it little thought, eyes closed, head nodding, fancying Jinx flushing quail to reality. The sirens were closer now, at the top of the hill by the Union Meeting House, heading into town.

The flashing red lights on the fire trucks came splashing through my front windows, bouncing off the fireplace jolting me back to the here and now. The sirens had stopped but the red lights had not. They did not pass by. Flashing and flashing filling the entire house. Panic filled every fiber of my being. Could sparks from my fire have set my neighbor's house on fire? Or what if the sixty-foot-tall Norway spruce downwind had caught fire? My imagination was running wild. I had had five or more Jack Daniels than I needed.

Someone was banging the brass knocker loudly on the front door. I staggered toward the door. Jack got there ahead of me, barking and jumping. The lock did not want to unlock. Be still my heart, I cussed it, the door opened.

"Merry Christmas," the volunteer fireman said, as he handed me a candy cane.

ONE LAST JOB

C.S. "Hunley" Johnson's call found me enjoying Happy Hour at the Tasting Room, in Frederick, that would make it a Friday. A long-standing tradition being faithfully observed. This one was the Friday before Memorial Day 2006.

Against my better judgement I hit "Accept. "
Was'up?
"I hired three new guys, good men, I've known them for years."
"How much?"
"They will work for $40. And we can bill $80."
"That's cool send me their info so I can pay them."
"We could use a couple more, why don't you come out, we can make you billable?"
"I don't know how to do commissioning and validation. I've never worked in the field"
"No problem, I'll show you how to do it. Fly out Monday, I'll get you into the hotel and pick you up at the airport."
"Hold on Hunley, ...Let me think on it ... Billy, may I have another

one, please." "Give me a minute, Hunley" Billy is really a good bartender, in less than a minute he has a fresh whiskey in front of me.

I've known Hunley for some years now and I should have known better. There is always one more question I should have asked. Hunley and I worked together at one of the world's largest engineering/construction firms. I headed up the pharmaceutical group out of Cleveland and he was in business development in Philadelphia. We worked well together and built a business from nothing into something when a merger left us looking for something else to do. Neither of us was very good at corporate politics. But we knew how to get business, and we did. Commissioning and validation had become the most expensive line item in the process of building a pharmaceutical plant. So, I transformed my old engineering company into a company that performed commissioning and validation. Somehow or another we landed a project in a burb of Seattle.

Memorial Day found me in the First-Class cabin of Northwest Airlines from Dulles to Seattle. Hunley picked me up and about 40 minutes later we arrived at an extended stay place that I had never heard of. At best, it could be described as semi comfortable with a nice outdoor pool

"We need to be at the job site at 6:00, I'll drive, meet me in the lobby at 5:30", we can get your Hertz car after work". After work was twelve hours later.

The biggest problem was the hotel didn't serve breakfast until 6: 00 am, and we were on the job site at 6:00 am. Six guys staying in this place for five months and they could not adjust their hours. This was not good. I'm not worth much without breakfast.

I'm jet lagged and tired.

I stayed that way all summer.

We needed more people on the job. I called C.J. Smith and asked him to join us. An engineer by education, he would be anal enough to be good at this job. He arrived in early June. He fit in very well, a duck to water.

The hotel is within walking distance of a respectable bar that served food. Turned out to be a local meet market for the over forty crowd. One night there, I was late and when I arrived C.J. who had been chatting up a semi over-served fortyish attractive lady, invited me to join them. The fortyish attractive lady excused herself and headed toward the rest room. Staggering and stumbling as she did so.
Upon her return, still staggering, I gave her an inquiring look.
"I can hold my liquor."
"How by the ears?" She thought about that for a moment, humor escaped her, and she hurried out the door.

I flew home over the 4th of July to incarcerate my mother in an assisted living place, long overdue, she failed the initial interview at a very nice place in Westminster, attitude problem, so I logged her into a place in Middleburg, where most everyone she knew went there to die. I guess if you know you're going to a place to die, it might as well be a place where you know people.
The real significance of this is that the family home of almost a hundred years is now vacant. It has been neglected for years. It needs work.
A routine of sorts settled in, twelve-hour days Monday through Friday, Saturday offered a break from the drudgery. We only worked six hours and then, oh joy, I got to play golf with our client and Hunley in the afternoon. Sunday was fun day. C.J. and I would start early, the damn hotel did not provide breakfast on weekends, searching out local wineries. Chateau St. Michel was five minutes away. The ferry to Whidbey Island was a short drive. We would have needed a month of Sundays to properly cover all the wineries. We discovered Whidbeys American Port; we bought the entire vintage.
By the end of summer, we had amassed eight cases of wine that we

had not yet consumed. I was way too tired, not feeling at all well. It was not that long ago that I was diagnosed with coronary artery disease. I was feeling my age, only a few months from Medicare.

The Wednesday before Labor Day Weekend, I bought Hunley dinner.

"I'm firing myself."

"Hang in, we will be finished by Thanksgiving."

"Sorry, but I'm tired and I think sick. I'm going home this weekend."

Shaking his head, "Is C.J. going with you?"

"No, he'll stay to the end." I had already had a seance with C.J. and we worked out a plan to get our wine back to Maryland.

"Suppose I buy a truck and drive it home."

'What kind of truck are you thinking about."

"I've always wanted a Range Rover."

The Sunday of Labor Day Weekend, we loaded eight cases of wine, golf clubs, and a couple of Sage fly rods that I bought on Saturday into the cargo area of a brand spanking new Range Rover.

On Labor Day itself, I headed my brand spanking new Range Rover west out of Seattle. Found myself a cabin overlooking Puget Sound, hired a fly-fishing guide, fished for steelhead in the morning, played golf at Meadowmeer Golf Club in the afternoon and treated myself to dinner at the best restaurants I could find. There was no shortage of great places to eat. Didn't like the guide, fired him on the second day, slept in for a couple of days, gave up golf, continued enjoying fabulous dinners at The Oyster & Thistle, with good whiskey and great local wine.

The end of each day found me perched on a stool, in a small neighborhood bar, at the short end of the bar's elbow, my back to a PBR neon sign, charming a leggy blond barkeep, with dark brown roots who wore her shirt unbuttoned enough to encourage an extra tip or two. Sweet lips, perky nose, dark round eyes that somehow sparkled, waspy waist and long shapely legs that ended at a bottom that did not need to be propped up on a pillow. She was a few years short of meeting the Hemingway standard.

The first rule of road tripping is: If you think you might want or need something bring it with you.

Despite all this fun, I still didn't feel up to snuff. What to do? The answer became obvious over a night cap with the leggy blond barkeep, with dark brown roots. I had gotten to know her some, didn't smoke, her hair smelled like wild lavender. When I told her that I have always been fascinated with the San Juan Islands, she said there is a ferry close by that can get you there, not us. She was almost persuaded. Something about the band of gold on my left hand.

Friday Harbor did not disappoint.

Charming, rustic, the harbor filled with the tall masts of sailing yachts, shops, restaurants and bars line the street and if you're not careful you might drive right through it without knowing it. It is a town for exploring on foot. I found a perfectly delightful inn on the outskirts, parked the truck and set out on foot to find the bar I drove past that overlooked the harbor.

I felt this place is different as I walked toward the harbor. It looked comfortable, pleasant with a lot of charm. The air was warm with a hint of salt and heavy on my skin. I was excited to be here. Downriggers became my go to place on those days that I could not walk past the Cask & Schooner.

Small, sweet, on the half shell, the best oysters I've ever tasted, served with Chateau St. Michel chardonnay. A warm sun blessing the patio, sail boats gently rolling in the blue water, respectable wine, fighting off thoughts of regret that the leggy blond barkeep with dark brown roots was not here.

Not to take anything away from Chesapeake Bay oysters, but these were exceptional. I don't know if they were Samish Bay, Olympias, or Kumamoto's as I was too busy enjoying them to ask. I tried other places to eat but I somehow managed to come back here at least once a day. I remember, I varied from the half-shell menu and tried Westcott Bay Oysters, baked, as a prelude to fresh pan-seared Halibut.

Leggy blond barkeep with dark blond roots would have enjoyed this.

I had bought a couple of cheap aluminum lawn chairs at a hardware store in Oak Harbor with hopeful thoughts that did not pan out. Most days were spent touring the island, looking for a perfect place to relax and breath in the scenery. There was no golf, no fishing, even though as I was driving around, I kept an eye out for a likely stream, but didn't find any appealing. The same thing can be said of the pickings at the local bars.

I parked the truck on the side of a narrow road, no evidence of civilization in sight. No tourists, no locals, no evidence that mankind existed, only a Magpie fussing about, for company. Unfolded one of the chairs, set it up on the shoulder of a grassy hill with wild lavender running toward the water's edge, a patch of poppies here and there, with Mount Rainier filling in the distant horizon. A pod of Orca's played a few yards offshore, could have been three or four. I awoke as the sun was falling behind the hill, setting the sky on fire, a chill had set in. More wine and oysters were soon enjoyed at Downriggers.

I don't remember how many days I was in Friday's Harbor, only that it was not enough. At some point, I decided I needed to visit Victoria, British Columbia. I leave Friday Harbor with a lonely, empty feeling. It would have been better if she would have come along.

There is a ferry, and there are customs, and there are hefty tariffs on wine, and I have eight cases.

Customs Station Inspector at ferry terminal, "May I see your passport and driver's license."

"Yes sir." I had them handy.

The officer peers curiously into the cargo area of the brand spanking new Range Rover. Taking my documents with him he walks slowly to the rear of the truck and opens the tailgate. Carefully, he surveys the eight cases of wine, golf clubs and the two Sage flyrods that were still strung up. He did not pay much attention to my luggage.

"Mr. West, do you have any business in Canada?"

"No sir, I'm just touring before heading home." I heard myself say this.

"Mr. West, do you have anything in this vehicle that you plan to leave in Canada."

"Well officer, there may be a golf ball or two that gets left behind, but nothing else."

"Have a nice day"

"Yes sir." Right foot hits floor.

Checked into the famous Fairmont Empress and set out to explore the beautiful Capitol District and harbor area. The flower beds are meticulously cared for, not a wilted blossom to be seen. There is no trash on the streets. There is no graffiti. The architecture is stunning. The area is magnificent.

I accidently stumbled into Murchies, a local landmark, for a fabulous lunch and a much-needed place to sit down and rest my feet. More urban trekking around the harbor, into Old Town, found a bookstore and bought a map *Back Roads of British Columbi*a, and over to Chinatown and back to the Empress, named for Queen Victoria, Empress of India.

I found my way into the Bengal Lounge tucked away in a far corner off the main lobby.

Plush.

British Raj. Elegant.

Gunga Din is here somewhere.

Maharaja, Ranjit Singh, is holding forth over a cadre of hangers-on in a private corner, far from the lobby. Rudyard Kipling is sipping a cup of tea, head buried in the latest edition of The Northern Star.

Peachy and Danny, legs crossed, pith helmets dangling from the toes of their knee-high leather boots, full dress uniforms, plotting some nefarious adventure, comfortable in tufted red leather sofas tucked in the corner with two lovely ladies draped in flowing sari, be-jeweled foreheads. Waiters in starched white Nehru jackets, creased black trousers bring Bengal Tiger martinis, stirred not shaken. Dark hardwood floors littered with oriental carpets. floor to ceiling columns encased in polished teak with brass sconces with a single candle, soft, romantic.

Slumped in an oversized leather sofa by the glowing fireplace, PH Jim Corbett, whisky in hand, chatted comfortably with "Papa", whose whisky was half gone. He gestured casually at the full stretched out skin and growling head of the man-eating tigress of Champawat, mounted above the hearth, mantel to ceiling. Champawat had claimed 436 victims before Corbett killed her after a harrowing stalk with two shots from his old black powder Martini Henry. Corbett specialized in only hunting tigers and leopards that were man eaters and always alone. There were on occasion, innocent victims. "Papa" gave a slow knowing smile and raised his glass in salute, emptied it, ordered another one.

A statue of a life size black panther stands guard by the entrance, a Raja Ravi Varma mural of sumptuous lake side India hangs over the bar. Most of the half dozen comfortable bar stools were unoccupied. Those that were, spilled an aroma of exotic curries and Bombay Stingers driving the nostrils to delusions. There are no unattached ladies.

Don't particularly like curry, nobody of interest at the bar, have had too much fish lately, needed a steak. Left the Empress found a steak house with a friendly bar, bourbon, struck up some conversation with locals, still no unattached ladies, learned the road to Whistler is one of the most scenic in the world.

On my way there I stopped by the Range Rover dealer and talked the service manager into teaching me how to operate the brand spanking new HSE. The road to Whistler is a narrow two-lane mountain trail bordering crystal blue lakes, reflecting snowcapped mountains and was being widened to accommodate traffic for the upcoming Winter Olympics. The scenery is truly distractingly beautiful. I was wishing for a designated driver.

Whistler was fairly well deserted. The summer people had gone home or back to school and the winter crew had not yet arrived. The shops, restaurants and bars had already jacked up their prices. I found the golf course, got paired with a guy and his girlfriend and a timber baron to round out the foursome. We were joined on the sixth tee by a lonesome coyote looking for a meal. He went about his business unhurried by our presence. Enjoyed a couple of beers with the timber baron, got a call from C.J. Smith, said I needed to sign some papers and would meet me in Vancouver in two days. He had been home to Maryland and went by my house to pick up waders, vest and other fly-fishing essentials. He'd bring them along.

C.J. found me at the Harborside Marriott at happy hour the second day. Said I looked tired. Told him I didn't feel well but could not put my figure on why. After a couple of drinks, we headed out of the Marriott. As we climbed up the hill on Albeani Street, we passed a two-story Chinese restaurant. The ground level was windowed, the cooks were making noodles by hand. C.J. insisted this was the place for dinner, we climbed the stairs to the mezzanine level and entered the restaurant proper.

We each ordered a whiskey to recuperate from walking up the hill and to bide some time while we surveyed the menu. Again, C.J. insisted we have the smoked tea duck and a delightful chardonnay. Our server, the one that brought the food, there were a bunch of others who did other stuff, was a very attractive oriental girl who told me she was spoken for or something to that effect and did I like my duck. I did indeed. To this day, C.J. says it was the best meal he has ever had. This from a man who spent years traveling the Far East lavishly, at our governments expense. It was memorable. I don't think either of us has ordered smoked tea duck anywhere else, knowing it would not measure up.

The next day must have been a Sunday. C.J. headed back to work with the signed papers, and I headed north to the backcountry with my fly-fishing gear.

Merritt is the Country Music Capitol of Canada; a few miles southeast is Corbett Lake Lodge. It was a lovely three-hour drive to the Lodge The lake and lodge are world-renowned as a fabulous fly-fishing destination. It is abundant with stocked Kamloops trout tipping the scales between twelve and eighteen pounds. They are why I came here.

The Lodge is nestled on three hundred acres of ponderosa pine, spruce, aspen and expansive wildflower meadows. There are no neighbors in sight. The rustic log lodge is perched on a knoll that provides panoramic views of Corbett Lake from the dining room and the lounge.

I arrived at the Lodge midafternoon, booked in for several days, settled into my room, and began to explore the property. I noticed a pier at the bottom of the hill stretching out into the lake. There were jonboats docked on both sides. It would be possible to cast a fly off the dock except there were other guests tossing bits of food to several very large trout.

Disappointed and disgusted, I headed for the bar.

Whatever ailment that has been plaguing me has raised its ugly head only worse this time. The next day instead of fishing I drove into Merritt. The town was quiet, no traffic, a few native Americans lounging about, the annual rodeo was last week. I found a pharmacist, described my symptoms, told him as a child growing up in The Orchard, I was susceptible to hay fever this time of the year. This malady did not feel exactly like The Orchard's hay fever which usually developed into asthma, but it was close. I walked out with a dozen pills of what, I don't know.

I stayed one more night at the Lodge. Did not make any friends, in fact, did not even strike up an interesting conversation with any of the other guests or the staff either. The pills helped some, could sleep all night. Could not figure out how to fish the lake, didn't feel well enough to cope with a boat, guide service was not available, decided to move on. Disgusted and disappointed with my experience at the Lodge.

The decision to not go to Banff was hard fought. I figured it would turn out to be like Friday Harbor, one of those places you need to be with someone special. So, I headed southeast, heading to the Elk River in Fernie, western slope cutthroat trout. Passed through some of the most spectacular scenery in the world, complete with the sighting of grizzly bears lounging in a meadow. There are not a whole lot of roads leading in this direction. The one I was on took me to Kelowna which unbeknownst to me is the home of some great wine. This was a total surprise and quickly put my miseries on a back burner. I think it is one of the most beautiful towns I've ever seen. Big blue lake surrounded by towering mountains with vineyards running downhill to the lake.

The country here is big, young, bold colors, rugged and reaches out a slaps you, saying," I am beautiful, love me". The countryside at home is older, softer, gentle shades of purple and green. It is subtle. It sneaks up on you, seduces your senses into a love affair.

I knew nothing of British Columbia wines. The architecture of Mission Hill Winery reached out and drew me in. Stunning arch way entrance and so are their wines. Pinot Noir is a favorite with Merlot their backup. Their restaurant was not open, but I managed several rounds of tastings and ended up spending more time and money here than I anticipated. I could not determine my favorite, so I bought two cases of each. Now I have twelve cases of wine in the boot.

There were still several hours of daylight remaining as I headed across the bridge out of town. Still two days to Fernie, passed through Penticton, Osoyoos, several inviting wineries, did not stop. Made it all the way to Castlegar, stopped for the night, very impressed with the cleanliness of all the towns and villages. There is no graffiti, no litter, everything is clean and well maintained.

Arrived in Fernie late afternoon the next day, checked into the Park Place Lodge

in the town center, a hop, skip, and jump from the Elk River Fly Shop. They provide guided float trips on the Elk River, native cutthroat on a dry fly, booked a half day trip starting the next afternoon. Perfect, I'm still sick, get to sleep late. Bret Mason introduced himself as being my guide. He is a strapping young fellow, rugged good looks and a devil-may-care attitude. He suggested some flies that might work, joined me for a beer at the hotel. Turns out to be a good guy, no toe ring, ski instructor in the winter, knows a bevy of local beauties.

We met at the fly shop after lunch, loaded my gear into his pickup, guide boat in tow, and headed north for about an hour to the put-in ramp. The rain began halfway there. Finally, a chance to use my new Sage 5#. Bret tied on a #6 Pink Lugger, barbless. It was cold, low forties and windy. The Elk was dark and fast. No need to cast, simply drop the fly on the water and a Cutthroat was on it like a New River smallmouth on cicadas. The action was fast and furious. The first one in the net was over twenty inches, fat and fought very hard, jumping and tail walking, a great fish. Hooked three more before I landed my second fish, all fought hard, shaking off the barbless hook. Two black bears fishing along the riverbank, took no notice. The rain had picked up, I was cold and getting wet. After we netted a couple more, I lost count, "hey Bret, how much longer till we get home?"

"About two hours."

"No way, put this thing in high gear, we're going home and drink some beer."

He did, and we did, and were joined by a couple of local lovely ladies. Checked off the bucket list western slope cutthroat, and possibly one other item. I don't know for sure her age.

It took much of the next day to get to Sweet Grass, Montana. Enough time to reflect, that I should have gone directly to Fernie from Victoria, or even directly from Seattle.

U.S. Customs inspector, after inspecting my papers, without checking the luggage area, "how long you been in Canada?"

"I don't know, what day is it."

"September 15th."

"About two weeks, I think."

Now he's looking at the, golf clubs, strung up fly rods, twelve cases of wine.

"Did you spend five thousand dollars?"

"Oh, good lord, no."

"Where you headed."

"Home." I heard myself say that again.

He walked to the front of the Range Rover and checked my license plate, Maryland.

Back at my rolled down window, "have a nice day."

Exited Customs slowly, with style, grace, and grateful.

Probably, should have stopped in Great Falls. The scenery was so beautiful I wanted to see it all now, not wait until tomorrow, afraid it might fade away. Did quit in Helena, found a Marriott, paid with points, met some interesting people and left the next morning.

C.J. Smith had plugged his home address into the GPS. It's ok, it's only twelve miles from beautiful downtown Frederick. The GPS woman who provides voice direction has a very annoying American accent, is way to bossy, sounds a lot like a wife. We had a violent confrontation near Billings good that I didn't have a gun. She wanted me to take I-94 which would take me to North Dakota and down to Chicago. I wanted to end up going through South Dakota and seeing Mount Rushmore. For whatever reason, I didn't get turned around soon enough, and was on I-94 heading east, passed near the Little Big Horn, highway signs warning of the dangers of meth, wide expansive prairie dotted with antelope, ended the day in Miles City. A great steak in a local bar was enjoyed with a group of locals all dressed in their finest Wrangler's, starched white shirt, black string tie, and black go to Sunday meeting Stetson's. There was a dance at the local fire hall. Barmaid found me a curiosity, never met anyone from out east.

Changed the American wife voice to a sweet, gentle, sophisticated British lady, found a back way to I-90 cross country to Gillette and on to Mount Rushmore. She didn't say "make a u turn" once.

There were still three more days of hard driving to beautiful downtown Frederick, Maryland.

Arrived just before happy hour, manually opened the garage door, backed the Range Rover into its new home, crossed the formal garden and entered the house via the kitchen door.

She was preparing some food, as a snack.

"Hello luv." Arms extended looking for a welcome home hug or a kiss even.

"Yea well, I'm leaving you."

Dropped arms, took a step back, "why the hell didn't you tell me that four days ago while I was still in Montana."

Walked slowly down to the Tasting Room, it must be a Friday. Kat will be there.

FEBRUARY 2007
38 EAST 2ND STREET
FREDERICK, MARYLAND

C.J. Smith and I were in the garage at the Frederick house loading stuff into the Range Rover. It was just stuff, nothing of note, but somehow Jack knew and found his way into the shotgun seat of the truck. C.J. opened the door get Jack out, Jack snarled, and C.J. closed the door. Jack was going wherever the Range Rover was going, come hell or high water. How he knew we were leaving for the last time, I don't know, but he knew.

Extensive fencing had been installed at The Orchard house, much to the displeasure of the neighbor and townsfolk in general. The yard was now escape proof. I had installed an automatic garage door opener, cut a pedestrian door in the side of the garage that lead to the garden. It was now possible to enter the garage, close the automatic door, let Jack out of the truck, and enter a totally fenced in yard. Jack's territory was secure. Carpenters had installed a doggie door on an outside wall of the house accessed from the pantry leading onto the patio. Jack could now come and go at his will.

Jack had never been to The Orchard. This would be his first experience with his new door and fenced yard. He found his door on his own and reconordered the fence, just in case there was an escape route. He knew he was home.

Jack had slept in the kitchen at the Frederick house. He made it plain he was not sleeping in the kitchen here. From the very first night, he placed himself between the bedroom door and the bed with his back to the bed and facing the door. Never wanted to sleep on the bed.

The Orchard became our new base of operation. We trained with Jeff Brooks at Brookwood Kennels every week. Jeff was working with Jack to run in field trials and was training me to handle him in the amateur trials. The next several years we were constant companions. We traveled to trials in Ohio, Wisconsin, New York, and closer to home in Pennsylvanian. Jack would ride to the trials in Jeff's truck and come home in mine. We were both living the life we were meant to live, and it was all good and fun.

FRIENDS CREEK
CATOCTIN MOUNTAINS, MARYLAND

Trout live in beautiful places.

Friends Creek meanders along and across the Mason-Dixon Line in the Catoctin Mountains, roughly between Antietam and Gettysburg. Camp David is over the next hill or two and Site R is around the corner. It is secluded, beautiful, and peaceful. It is one of those places that unless you have been there you don't know where it is. The stream is narrow with brier bushes and trees overhanging both banks. A series of waterfalls and riffles run for about a mile and a half. They form twenty-six named, deep pools that sometimes hold fish over from one year to the next. Several families from Washington's elite legal and intelligence community established the Friends Creek Anglers Association some fifty years ago. Some original members still fish here. It is private water, members and guests only, occasionally violated by local poachers. The one hundred sixty acres through which it flows is privately owned. The landowner tolerates the anglers and does not countenance the shooting of poachers.

This chilly April morning a chorus of spring gobblers greeted my friends and I as we arrived before the sun had burned the dew off the grass and continued the chorus until they got wind of our being there. Ben Franklin claimed turkeys can't smell but they hear darn good.

Today, the stream was high, fast, and just a little clear. She would likely give up her trout grudgingly. It is a catch and release stream, fly-fishing only.

Mike thought he might try for the brook trout that had been stocked two weeks ago in Pennsylvania's part of the creek, so he headed downstream to try Hogan's Pool at the very end of the property. The Alder Pool was Hill's choice; it is the biggest and widest and has always proved to hold a lot of fish. It is a difficult hole to fish but big enough that two anglers, one at top of the pool and the other at the bottom can cast freely without confrontation. I decide to join Hill and took up a position on a rock outcropping at the top of the pool. The water enters the pool fast and foamy, flowing over a long steep riffle before flattening out. I left Hill to wade in from the bottom and cast upstream into a wide expanse of deep slow water.

Casting a San Juan Worn into the swift flow brought no results, possibly because at some point the fly had freed itself and I was casting a naked tippet. Not to be deterred by stupidity, a large Woolly Bugger replaced the worm. I plopped a short cast in the current upstream and started stripping out some line when suddenly the slack was gone, and the line was headed rapidly downstream. A nice shiny rainbow had swallowed the fly whole. While trying to extricate the Woolly Bugger, the line broke, leaving the fly hooked into the fish's gullet I released the trout back into the water and said a little prayer for him. Cursed myself profusely. Began gathering my line to tie on another fly and notice that the top four inches of my 4# bamboo rod was dangling at right angles to the other eight feet. Resumed cursing.

I advised Hill of this tragic situation and told him I had a spare tip at the Nutshell but would go upstream to fish the Swimming Hole upon replacement of the broken one.

The Nutshell is a well-maintained, oversized hut perched high above the stream that provides almost all the comforts of home. An FCAA member angler can book it for overnight stays by phoning an administrative assistant at the Supreme Court of the United States. Kat and I have established a tradition here. It has very nice sized bunk beds, baseboard heat, an electric stove with an oven even pots and pans. In the summer there is running water to the sink and the toilet. A small table has ample space for four place settings and looks out through large, clear, glass patio doors onto a large wooden deck that rises fifteen feet above the aptly named Nutshell Pool. The deck is a well-aged brown. The hut is painted a dark green. On the downstream side it is surrounded by redbud trees that are now in bloom, joined by just a couple more on the upstream side, next to large sycamore trees.

If the side facing the creek is the front side, then from the back there are ten uneven stone steps curling down and under the deck to a sandy patch of beach where you can easily cast a fly to the ripple above the Kilimanjaro rock. The rocks around the stairway are covered with tiny, pointed, blue-eyed grass.

The Kilimanjaro rock in the middle of the Nutshell Pool resembles a snow-covered volcano. Its sun-bleached tip rises above the water line, and if its point is underwater, the creek is likely not fishable. Despite heavy rains yesterday, a good four inches of the rock shone above the pool this morning. Standing on the deck we could see some fish hanging out by the Kilimanjaro rock. Downstream, a pair of mallards rose off Craig's Pool and flew upstream to where some golden trout had been spotted in the Swimming Hole.

A stair step of three waterfalls roars into the Swimming Pool. It is deep and dark, bordered on one side by a tall rock cliff perfect for a cannonball dive on a hot summer day, which it was not today. I realized it may be a tad too early in the season for fishing with a dry fly. The trout will not likely not be looking up for a meal just yet. I have caught my full share of trout here. If the good Lord allows me to catch another, I wish it to be on a dry fly. Concentrate, feel the wind, the flow pushing against your boots, where will the big ones likely be holding? I was on the rocky point at the western end where the flow from the falls cascades into the pool. It quickly forms a foam line that doesn't slow down until it runs into the rock cliff and turns left, some thirty feet later. I cast a dry fly, a small, nearly always reliable yellow and white parachute stimulator, bounced it off the cliff, and let it drift on the foam line. My third cast presented a temptation that a big brown could not resist. He put up a nice struggle. The trick is to turn them without breaking off. It requires a certain amount of patience gained through experience. This one was released back into the dark water without harm. My heart was pumping fast. The fishing gods may have forgiven me or figured a broken bamboo rod was penitence enough. I must have been a little too excited and forgot to pay attention; my very next cast hooked a tree branch twenty feet back and up. The gods were not yet finished with me.

As I walked toward the tree reeling in the line, my feet got tangled up; this can happen on dry flat land it does not need be in a swift-running stream with slippery wet rocks. The beaver stick wading staff was tied to my belt, but the knot came loose, and it went downstream.

Mike and Hill were downstream, likely more than a mile away, and it was early. I was alone. If I had fallen into the water it wouldn't have hurt too bad, but I did not. Instead, I went backward onto some very large and jagged rocks. Everything happened in slow motion, as things seem to do with the advancement of age. As I was falling, the branch let loose of the fly and it flew past me on my way down, still tied on the end of the line. It hit the ground before I did. The first thought that went through my head was the weather might have been just a tad too cool for the copperheads.

Somehow, I ended up with my knees higher than my buttocks; waders and heavy boots became an anchor. I was wedged in, could not get up or turn over. Struggling to get the leverage needed to roll over and get my feet back under me seemed to take forever, and I wasn't at all sure it was too cool for the copperheads. They became my main fear once I realized nothing was broken. Hurt, yes; maybe a cracked rib or two, maybe my spleen. I needed to get out of where I was. There was green moss covering a large rock to my right, by my head. I thought if I could get a hand on it, I could leverage myself out of the wedge. Green moss in an open wound… oh well. I finally rolled over and got my knees where God meant them to be, with my feet below them. Both of my hands were bleeding; maybe I cut them on the mossy rocks struggling to turn over. I looked around and found my beaver stick floating in the pool; it has special meaning, two casts later, I'd fished it in.

There are about two hundred yards of gravel lane back to the Nutshell where we had stashed our gear. It took all of thirty minutes to get myself there and stop the bleeding. Grimacing, as putting one foot in front of the other caused shooting stabs of pain throughout my back; was it organic or structural, or an aggravation of an old problem? Thirty minutes of self-incrimination followed: Would anyone have heard three short, three long, three short blasts on my emergency whistle, which was still tucked in my vest pocket? Would they have thought it was Morse code or a songbird? How long do you pause before repeating the SOS? It matters not. I forgot I even carried it, much less remembered to tell anybody else to be alert for it. I was still worrying over the snakes.

No one was at the Nutshell, so I made a bandage out of my red and white kerchief. I administered the first aid as best I could and waited for Hill or Mike to show up for lunch—in about two hours. A local who deer hunts the property stopped by to see if he could get permission to hunt mushrooms, but the owner was not there. Hill got there about the same time as the mushroom hunter and was the first to come for lunch. He had some proper antiseptic and bandages. The deer hunter had some proper adhesive tape. The wounds were cleaned, but nothing wanted to move.

Mike finally arrived for lunch. "Want some ibuprofen? I have some."

"No, thanks."

"Beer would be better."

Mike unpacked the lunch, unconcerned that I thought I might die. He pulled out a nice tablecloth to cover the old wooden picnic table on which I had been resting. Lunch would have provided more than what ten hungry folks could have eaten and enough wine for all ten. There were only three of us. The deer hunter had given up on the owner returning and gone home.

My friend Martin arrived with a bottle of wine as we were slowing down with the food. He was unaware of and remained totally oblivious to my plight. His social life would not accommodate his rising early in the morning.

He sampled some cheese, declared it very good, and began to pull on his waders. Stringing up his rod, he asked advice as to what fly was working. I told him my dry fly worked but damn near killed me. The trout were not rising, so maybe a nymph might be a good idea.

What was left of lunch was packed up and put in Hill's Chevy Suburban, including the tablecloth, allowing me to resume my flat-on-my-back position, lifting myself on one elbow for a sip of wine every now and again. The beer was gone. I did not pee blood. The clouds had lifted, and the sun began to warm the air.

Mike and Martin went downstream hoping for a hatch on the Alder Pool. Hill thought he'd go upstream to try his luck in the Swimming Pool; it had been left quiet for a couple of hours. I tried to take a nap. "Maybe I'll just not wake up," I thought, but I only succeeded on and off.

The sun felt good enough that, after some time, I figured I'd try to get down to Alder Pool. I still had my waders and boots on, but it was a painful walk. Mike was having a good afternoon. He gave me his camera, and I documented some big trout in his net. I tried casting from the bank to a pod of trout about twenty feet out, hiding around a submerged log. A couple of casts and I hooked the only tree I could have, slipped and fell again, not so hard this time. Mostly I just slid down the bank to the water's edge, saved the fly, and went back to the picnic table.

Hill never made it to the Swimming Pool. He stopped at the Swinging Bridge Pool. There is no longer a bridge of any kind, though there once was it led to a path that ran up the hill to a log cabin which is now falling down. It is a difficult spot to access. He had to climb down a steep, rock-littered bank, over and around some big boulders, to get into a position to cast to the deep pool where the trout might live, and where I had spotted a very large copperhead last year. He found that four big rainbows called this hole home. He released them, so they still do.

The sun was slipping behind the mountain to the west; dusk was about to settle over the creek. I heard Martin wading upstream, casting in pools that are generally empty of fish. He stepped into the shallow end of the Nutshell Pool, crouched down, lowering his profile. He moved slowly and quietly and cast the line into the current, just above the Kilimanjaro rock; a very nice rainbow became the last fish caught that day.

Mike grilled the steaks to perfection. Cigars were lit on the deck. A quite delicious vintage port was decanted. It was the last bottle of my collection of Pacific Northwest port, good, very aromatic, and pleasantly sweet. If I'm going to die tonight…

Mike flicked the ash off the end of his cigar, which landed where his steak once was, just missing what was left of his dessert. Time to go home.

"Is there more port?" I asked. "Never mind; I'll switch back to whiskey."

Raising a final salute, I solemnly vowed to never fish along again.

NOVEMBER 24, 2013
BAY POINT, PANAMA CITY BEACH, FLORIDA
THANKSGIVING QUAIL

Jack became another heartbeat in my home in July 2003. Age eight weeks. On the Friday after the Monday my most recent ex-wife told me I could not have another dog. I had been without a field-bred Springer for about two years, which was way too long.

The choice to spend this winter in Panama City Beach came about largely because Jack was no longer with me. The departure from this life of the only living one in the whole world you love…who loves you back… leaves an emptiness in the depths of my soul.

Jack will forever be in my heart. The loneliness is replaced with memories of the joy he brought to my life, and that joy recalls the times afield with Smoke and Remy. It is a good state of mind. At some point, it dawns on me that this is the first time in over forty years that I've no responsibility to another living soul. I am free and free I shall live.

I'm in Panama City Beach not because I'm well off or well into being a septuagenarian and need not to be cold, or because of the beautiful sugar white beaches. Nor is it my hope of finding another rich widow to keep me warm. But rather, my very good friend J.R. Pruitt lives in Albany, Georgia. He moved here about four years ago, shortly after we both joined Friends Creek. We have hunted, fished, and sometimes even golfed together for almost twelve years, and southwest Georgia is the bobwhite quail hunting capital of the world. His son-in-law and daughter own a condo on the beach, so he visits regularly. Maybe I am looking for a new beginning to the rest of my life.

The first eight of those twelve years we both lived in Frederick, Maryland. Just about every Friday at five o'clock, beginning in 2001, J. R. joined Flynn McPherson and me in our long-standing tradition of happy hour at Brewer's Alley. These gatherings were much anticipated, so much so that from time to time we moved them up to Wednesday. The trials and tribulations of the business day were put aside, and discussion was more concerned with the fun we had last week and where we were going to have fun next week.

Flynn, J.R., and I hunted and fished together every chance we could. The first was a spring float trip on the North Branch of the Delaware in 2002. Jeremiah Reddy Pruitt, J.R. for short, is proudly from West Virginia, his momma gave him Jeremiah, because she loved the Bible. Reddy was his grandfather's mother's maiden name and the Pruitt's have been in West Virginia since before coal. The one leg is shorter than the other jokes will raise a hackle. The retort is not pretty. Whatever bar it was that we ended up in, the patrons noticed that J.R.'s accent was different from theirs. It was tense for a while, until the guides we had been fishing with intervened when they realized Flynn had not yet paid them. Nobody ever called him "Red" more than once.

By the fall of 2002, the three of us had logged fond memories of trout on Pennsylvania's spring creeks, South Carolina's quail, redfish, and some other pleasures or two. There were two days in Bimini where a Mexican kid conned Flynn out of his Rolex. We had a few drinks too many in the Complete Angler Hotel, a Hemingway favorite. It housed a wonderful collection of his memorabilia before it burned to the ground four years after our visit. That was before the two weeks in Europe for business, if Oktoberfest can be considered business. The City of Munich ran out of Gentlemen Jack and ice. I was buying time, she was selling times, once was not enough. A three-day float trip in October on the Deschutes in Oregon was physically demanding. Flynn declared his steelhead was bigger than mine. It was his dime. He dropped his first glass of gin then.

Brain tumor.

Three months later in January 2003, a biopsy confirmed the diagnosis at the Mayo Clinic, Minneapolis. The treatment consultation at Hopkins in Baltimore was devastating. Flynn, his wife, and I met with the doctor who was the head of the brain cancer group and ten other employees who had nothing to do with brain cancer but were there to cover for malpractice insurance. The head brain cancer doctor described the treatment as twelve months of radiation and chemotherapy, after which you will think the tumor has been defeated and you will feel cured. You will be wrong. No one has ever been cured. All we will have done is piss it off and it will come back with a vengeance. There will be nothing we can do, and you will die in three months. Fifteen months later he left a very lovely and very rich widow.

Brain cancer is nasty shit. The treatment ended happy hours. The hours were no longer happy, and so our get togethers were suspended. Brewer's Alley beer no longer tasted the same. J.R. spoke from the altar at the memorial service. I wore sunglasses. We both carried him out and laid him to rest.

After Flynn's passing, J.R. and I moved our charm, wit, and personalities, to say nothing of good looks, to The Tasting Room just across and down Market Street. J.R. says he lost his looks after leaving Charles Town and moving to Dallas. It is most likely a good thing, could have been shot had he stayed in Charles Town. The TR did not have draft beer, instead fancied itself a martini bar. During happy hour the cost between a beer and Jack Daniels was not worth mentioning, and the pour was respectfully generous. It was there that I first met Kat.

J.R. moved to Albany in 2009, but I continue the tradition of happy hour every Friday to this day. And when I do meet up with J.R., no matter where we are or how long since we've been together, the first drink is a "Cheers Flynn."

NOVEMBER 25, 2013
ALBANY, GEORGIA
THE PRUITTS' HOUSE

I have only been at Bay Point four days, and there's nothing I don't love about it. It is not The Orchard. J.R. and Julie Pruitt invited me to Thanksgiving dinner, which has become a tradition for the past seven years, maybe even before that. When I was still married sometimes it was at my house, sometimes at their house, no matter where we lived. Then they pretty much adopted me after the most recent ex-wife left, and Thanksgiving was of course at their house.

It is good to love and be loved.

J.R. thought quail on the grill would be a pretty good warm-up on Thanksgiving Eve for the turkey waiting to be the main course on Thanksgiving Day. I booked us into Riverview Plantation for half a day's hunt on Tuesday, including lunch and a guide. I arrived in Albany on Monday in time for happy hour, checked myself into the Pruitt's guest room, and found my way to J.R.'s supply of whiskey. J.R. thinks bourbon tastes like kerosene and will not drink anything he can see through.

Dinner was at the country club and as always was a treat. They give a good pour, and the food is great and one of the waitresses' kind of likes me. A winter storm arrived about the same time I did and dumped three plus inches of rain on Georgia and a foot of snow on The Orchard. I love the South. Riverview moved our reservation back a day without a problem.

**NOVEMBER 26, 2013
CAMELIA, GEORGIA
RIVERVIEW PLANTATION**

Cader Cox IV greets us in the clubhouse of Riverview Plantation, a four-generation family operation and with at least one more on the way. A wood fire in the stone fireplace takes the chill off a cool Georgia day. There is the scent of rich dark leather with a hint of bourbon. An oriental rug rests on the wide plank heart of pine floor. Hunting scenes hang on the dark wall paneling; brass and copper accents complete a warm welcome. It feels like we have been here before. We settled into one of the leather couches as Cader IV introduces us to Cader III for the mandatory safety video and lecture. Apparently, some Type A personalities from up north suffer an unacceptable number of accidents upon the guides, dogs, and even their hunting partners. We assure Cader III that we are safe and gentlemen shooters and anybody who shoots a dog deserves jail time, if he is indeed not shot first. The obligatory stuff out of the way, we are shown to a private dining room for lunch.

Ah, lunch — or dinner, as it's known in the South.

Every quail plantation there is say they offer traditional quail hunting and honest-to-God Southern food. Retha does; she runs the kitchen and cooks the food. She has blessed us with the absolute most wonderful chicken 'n dumplin's that only your grandmother's mother might rival. A side of indescribably good grilled pimento cheese sandwiches, complemented by an old-fashioned rendition of blueberry cobbler, the best ever to grace a southern table, all to die for, and sweet tea.

We should have said grace. Next time, Lord. We have been transported to an earlier time and place, and it feels good.

The Hunt

J.R. Pruitt is not tall, his blacksmith arms and a nine-month belly that bulge under his blaze-orange shooting shirt. His gray, well-trimmed moustache on a rugged face that some women find handsome portrays a dapper shooter to our guide Jarvis and the assembled other sportsmen. His demeanor suggests that he has been on a proper quail plantation before.

J.R. is half a decade plus some younger than me, and a tad more agile. Not a lot, but some. A bad back brought on by age and the wages of sin requires an almighty effort for Jarvis to load me onto the elevated bench seat in his open, custom-designed Jeep just ahead of his six dogs, who are quietly settled into their kennels. J.R. is settled in on the shotgun side, and off we go into Georgia's longleaf pines.

It does not take long for his beautiful English Setters, white with some black ticking and ears, tail feathers dancing in the breeze, to come to point.

Sam and Pebbles look to be related. Pebbles gets the first point, staunch, tail held high, stretched out long and low. Sam honors, and Jarvis kicks up a small covey. Four barrels are emptied; there are now three less than there were before. Jarvis handles Sam and Pebbles in the retrieve of the dead birds. Both dogs had good marks and the retrieving did not take long. The first shots out of the box are important to a sport's credibility with a guide. As the third bird tumbles down some good ways off, a "good shot" from Jarvis sets the tone for three hours more of the same.

I was shooting my German-made sixteen gauge, a gift from the Widow Mc Pherson. I had recently sold my best quail gun, a 20-gauge Philadelphia Fox. It was one of those guns that when you hold it for the first time it jumps up and kisses you on the cheek. This is the same gun that Ph.D. Penelope damn near killed me, the trapper, and herself with in the Grouse Butt at Hill Country Hunt Club a year or so ago. She had broken her first clay pigeon, she turned around to acknowledge the cheers, lowering the gun as she turned, and the second barrel discharged missing the stone butte by inches. The safety was manual. She forgot.

Ph.D. Penelope, a fine English lass of high intellect, fancied she wanted to learn to shoot. She looks like what you might think a young English woman with a Ph.D. in microbiology might look like, except she has a kick-ass body. I found her to be quite lovely when I met her at a pharmaceutical event about three years ago. Even though she said she was engaged to some guy in England, we managed several days a week together for over a year. This fun was interrupted briefly so she could fly to Las Vegas and marry the guy, but was promptly resumed upon his return to England, leaving her in Frederick.

After a long while, my back quit working altogether. I can hardly walk, cannot get in or out of the Jeep, cannot sit and stretch. There were large coveys and smaller coveys and picking up singles, and I asked, "Does your dog point snakes?"

"No." I am not clear as to what followed; t'was unintelligible…

"Look out for that anthill, come over here; let me check your boots, see if you got any." Jarvis propped my foot on the Jeep's running board and knocked off two stragglers.

The shadows grow longer; me 'n' J.R. are done in, limit filled. Only

Sam and Pebbles want more. I never hunted quail with Jack; probably nobody has hunted quail with a flushing dog after the first guy tried. Pheasants, grouse, even waterfowl, but not quail.

There are plenty of quail for dinner tonight, and I have enough to take a bunch back for an elk and quail dinner on my birthday later at The Orchard. J.R. and I have hunted on other quail plantations in the area before. We will go back to Riverview. It was all good and fun.

We drive back to Albany tired and an hour late for happy hour, so there was lots of time to make up. We did.

J.R.'s daughter and son-in-law have gone to the Biltmore for Thanksgiving, leaving J.R. and Julie to stay at the plantation house and I to stay at their home just a few minutes away. Jake, Shannon's dog, enjoys their company. I don't mind being left alone with J.R.'s whiskey. He fixed the quail as an appetizer; all I'm allowed to reveal is it's marinated in buttermilk, goes well with a fine Oregon Pinot Noir.

A twenty-one-pound turkey is being prepared for tomorrow's dinner.

THANKSGIVING DAY, 2013
ALBANY, GEORGIA
SHANNON AND GRANT'S PLANTATION HOUSE

Julie and J. R., Franz and Mandy, and me.
    We said grace.
    It is good to love and be loved.

DECEMBER 5, 2013
BAY POINT, PANAMA CITY BEACH, FLORIDA

The winter storm that dumped a foot of snow on Maryland did me no favors.

The original plan was to head from Bay Point to Cambridge, Maryland. The cocktail party at the National Open English Springer Spaniel Field Trial

Championship was being sponsored by my old friend, Jerry Caccio. He trained Smoke back in the '80s. I needed to be there. He claims I've already had the best dog I'll ever have. My many new friends out of the Brookwood Kennels training sessions will also be there. The forecast called for a big snowstorm and changed my route to go directly to The Orchard, picking up I-75 in Atlanta to Knoxville. I checked into the big Marriott on the river, too late and too far from the wine bistro to see the lovely and incredible Robin.

DECEMBER 7, 2013
THE ORCHARD

The storm didn't amount to much in Cambridge, but I would not have made it to The Orchard on Sunday in time for my elk and quail birthday dinner. My friends Martin and Kat, and Martin's person of interest, were to pre-prepare the elk. I had the quail marinating in buttermilk with me; both were to be grilled on-site. Jonnie and Jamie were to bring wine and cigars. A person should celebrate their birthday with friends, even if it is in The Orchard.

Nobody could make it Sunday. It was still snowing on Monday, so we postponed until Tuesday. Only Martin from the original guest list showed, and I added C.J. Smith. He only lives twelve miles away, has a four-wheel drive, a heart of gold, and no objection to a free meal. Small-batch bourbon started the festivities. Martin grilled everything, and it was better than good. Judging from the number of empty wine bottles left on the table the next morning, a good time was had by all. My last bottle of fabulous port from the great Northwest was among the dead. Don't remember if there were cigars.

The good news is that I have some delicious leftovers to enjoy here in Florida. I could not leave The Orchard soon enough. I arrived in Bay Point Thursday afternoon, having stopped in Knoxville for some dinner. I did not go by the wine bistro to see the lovely and incredible mixologist Robin. Same excuse as before.

Winter storms be damned!

DECEMBER 17, 2013
BAY POINT, PANAMA CITY BEACH, FLORIDA
WILD DUCK GUMBO

The mornings are chilly, warming to the sixties in the afternoon. I have been invited to spend Christmas with J.R. and his family in Albany. J.R. thought it would be nice to have duck gumbo on Christmas Eve. The last time he had a similar idea was back in 2008, when he thought it would be a good idea to bring white chili to the Annual Friends Creek Anglers Association picnic. It was our first picnic as members, and J.R. wanted to make a good impression.

He hired a duck hunting guide, Hicks, for two half days. For the white chili he wanted to use pheasant, which was to be harvested at Hill Country Hunt Club, a sporting club I joined along with Jack that offers pheasant shooting and deer hunting near Blue Ridge Summit, Pennsylvania. There may not be a wild pheasant left in Pennsylvania. I hired the guide and his dogs; Jack was in training for field trialing, and I would have been flogged for taking him rough hunting. I invited two other shooters. We needed a lot of chili. A dozen or so birds were pointed by English Setters, brought down with number six shot, and retrieved by an English Cocker. It was expensive.

J.R. had used Hicks to guide him fly-fishing last summer and is not crazy about his boat. We arrived at the appointed location at 4:30 a.m., a little late, for which we were roundly chastised.

We had to motor forever over a very choppy East Bay in a small eighteen-foot flat-bottom aluminum boat, without the comfort of a single cushion or bench. Bouncing on the rough water rearranged most of my innards. For no apparent reason, Hicks decided to drop anchor, build a blind of palmetto fronds, and set the decoys.

We anchored off a point of land where there were other hunters with head lamps also building a blind. Hicks found their location stupid; it would be out of the water when the tide went out in an hour. He hollered across the water to tell them exactly how stupid they were. Exactly what they hollered back was not clear, but it was angry. And when they shot at a flock of very high-flying ducks before legal shooting hours, the hollering got to be a bit scary. We were out of shotgun range. Charlie, his Black Lab, was romping in the shallow water chasing crabs and shorebirds, and his safety was of concern. All this before the sun rose to a cloudless sky and a fifteen-knot wind out of the north.

A big, high, blue sky and more wind than desirable did not bode well for a successful hunt. Hicks said there were a thousand Redheads there yesterday. Every no-good guide says the same. He had a dozen duck calls hanging from his neck. He never presented evidence that any of them were operational. He claimed not to wear a toe ring. It was too cold to find out for sure, but he had all the symptoms of a guide that would, lots of glitz.

We spent the morning covered with the palmetto fronds and dressed in camo. J.R. had camo waders and got in the water, helping to plant the fronds in the mud bottom. I did not have waders, just L.L. Bean's best cold-weather camo, so I stayed in the boat. Don't think I'll get waders for next year.

It is extremely difficult to hit a fast-flying anything, much less a small duck, while rocking in ten- to twelve-knot winds in a small boat. By nine o'clock we managed to adjust enough so that we could make a small serving of Bufflehead gumbo for Christmas Eve.

Day two brought better weather; we were on time, had less wind, and there were more ducks. No Redheads, just low and fast Buffleheads. Charlie, two years old, tips in at ninety pounds. He is in his spot on the forward port side of the boat, ever vigilant for incoming. He is a smart dog. He knows when the guns fire, birds likely need to be brought to hand. He was in the water in a heartbeat, just forgot to wait and see where they fell. Hicks spent a lot of time in the water providing direction. He became a decent retriever himself. Never did pick up a cripple; out of the boat with his gun, waist deep, missed it three times. If he'd had more shells, he'd have missed it more. Charlie saw it and headed to go get it but was called off. And somehow, another one was lost that was at one-point dead in the boat. J.R. can now make a good-sized pot of gumbo.

DECEMBER 23, 2013
CHRISTMAS WITH THE PRUITTS
ALBANY, GEORGIA

It was happy hour when I arrived at J.R.'s house a day before Christmas Eve. I checked into the guest room. J.R. has had a heart episode, so there's a new house rule that only applies to J.R. His daughter Shannon is a doctor. She loves him, as does his wife, Julie, who enforces the rule. No spirits before five o'clock. But it's Christmas almost, and the rule only applies to J.R. Julie poured me a generous whiskey. J.R. pouted. Dinner was at Doubletree Country Club, with a very good chef, and they poured a proper drink.

Christmas Eve dawns clear, bright, and very comfortable, with just a light sweater needed.

My job was to stay out of the way; after years of experience, I've become quite accomplished at it. Just as they had done with the pheasants, J.R. and Julie handpicked through the cooked duck breasts in search of number six steel shot. J.R. was extra careful. At the Friends Creek Dam Day picnic, J.R. had served all but the last scoop of chili to the esteemed members and guests, getting fantastic reviews. He had saved the last scoop for himself. In the first bite, he found a single missed number six and broke a tooth. It is now called the Five Thousand Dollar White Chili.

Once satisfied they had found all the shot J.R. and Julie added the meat to the roux. They had done the same for the picnic.

Dinner was at Shannon and Grant's plantation house just two miles from J.R. and Julie's home. Franz and Mandy, Jack and Carol were there. I'd met them at previous celebrations, nice folks. There was a boundless supply of Jack Daniels and great wine. There was plenty of wonderful duck gumbo. There were no leftovers.

CHRISTMAS DAY
THE PRUITTS'
ALBANY, GEORGIA

Julie said the blessing
    It is good to love and be loved.

JANUARY 23, 2014
GOOSE CAMP
STILL POINT POND
NEAR CHESTERTOWN, MARYLAND

This is the first year I've been aware of that winter storms have been given names. How long has this been going on? Do they have a gender?

There are some things in life that are more important than others. Being a part of tradition is one of those important things. Tradition adds continuity and substance to life, transcending a mere existence. No matter how comfortable I am in Bay Point or how difficult it might be to get to Maryland, it is essential I join my longtime friends for our annual hunting trip. The group includes Ron and Mike Wright, both architects by education but neither in practice for a living, and Mike's father-in-law, Hill Mason, Attorney at Law (Ret.). We rent a house on Still Point Pond. They have now dubbed it Goose Camp. Everybody gets their own bedroom and private bath. This is our fourth year of hunting geese together and our second year at this house. I have hunted pheasants with Mike and Ron before, once with Mike in his native North Dakota with Jack the dog. Mike and Hill field dress the geese, saving the breasts for appetizers wrapped in bacon and grilled, maybe the best way to enjoy goose. Ron oversees grilling, it's salmon tonight and steaks tomorrow.

We do not go into Chestertown except for a forgotten grocery item or to replenish the adult beverage supply. I would enjoy the ambience of this lovely Eastern Shore town for cocktails. Meet some local talent for future reference, but my driving record is such that I need to enjoy happy hour at Goose Camp. A tradition for Wild Turkey 101 has been established. Hill and I are of the same age, and our palettes are more sophisticated, so ardent spirits are required. Jack Black is in the bullpen. Mike and Ron, being of an enlightened generation, imbibe in red wine, good and expensive red wine. Sleeping was not a problem that night, or any other for that matter, for any of us.

We hunt out of Cody's Goose Haven Farm. He had the guides set up some decoys on a frozen pond near a snow-covered corn field. It was about 200 yards from their nice warm barn headquarters. Cody said we were to be there at 9:30 a.m. So, we were, as were his son Shane and his black Lab, Deke. The air temperature was 10 degrees. A stiff breeze from the west made for a wind factor that was freaking cold. I am not a very experienced goose hunter. Three times before in Maryland and once in Maine. But I have heard it said that geese do not like to fly when it is cold, and the sky is blue and high. All of which it was that day.

There were four of us in the blind, and the geese should have been coming in from the east as they like to land into the wind. Well, every now and again, our guide would call in a single lonely goose that would come down seeking the company of our decoys. The problem was that us shooters were all lined up in the blind east to west, facing north, with me being on the far west end. So, by the time the goose would get to where I could shoot at it, it was already dead, and I was cold. Without having fired a shot in about two hours and our limit not half filled yet, Deke had damn little to do. I retreated to the wood-burning stove in the barn and stayed there the rest of the day. Have I mentioned that I'm of a different generation? Apologies to Hill, but he was, after all, a Philadelphia lawyer. My fellow shooters braved the elements and limited out about mid-afternoon. This is when the geese started flying because it warmed up some. Deke got busier.

Saturday was much better, warmer and a low sky. We were to be in the blind at the same time, and we were, under protest. It wasn't that much warmer. Cody said it would be okay. The setup was different this time. We were all facing east over a different snow-covered corn field. Flocks of up to six or eight geese came in over a strand of woods, straight at the blind. We limited out well before noon, and I had the left quadrant and satisfied my limit for both days. My 12-bore Benelli, a gift from the Widow McPherson, is better for modern hunting regulations than my Philadelphia Fox, which I prefer to shoot. Since it was not designed for steel shot, sacrifices to tradition were made. Two slow shots are sometimes more productive than three fast ones. I don't remember much about dinner that night; best my guess is it was pretty much like the night before.

JANUARY 28, 2014
BAY POINT
PANAMA CITY BEACH, FLORIDA

It's in the mid-twenties when I wake up. The morning sun reflects on a dead-still Upper Lagoon; the tide is out. The east waters of the Upper Lagoon show like polished steel as they cut toward the Intercoastal then on to the Gulf. My osprey is taking his first of the day on a limb of a tall dead tree just a few yards off my balcony. If only I should catch fish that big. I'm happy to be in Bay Point and have no plans to leave until the end of February.

I figured out how to work the DVD player. The TV is still a mystery, so I walk over to Club 19 if there is a game, I'm interested in. I've read everything written by Sir Arthur Canon Doyle and watched every one of Basil Rathbone's portrayal of Sherlock Holmes. It will warm to the high sixties. I will take my daily walk and contemplate life while enjoying the comings and goings of the lagoon life and this weekend, a little golf?

It is good to love and be loved, if only a little.

WINTER 2014
CHRISTMAS WITH KAT
A FRIENDS CREEK TRADITION INTERPTED

It is officially a tradition. Kat and I go fly fishing on Friends Creek every Christmas, almost. Friends Creek is a beautiful mountain stream and has a long and illustrious history, some really nice 'bows and browns, and a good deal of privacy.

The creek is truly mystical in the snow. The whole thing started the Christmas after my most recent ex-wife left. Kat was more than just a lovely young server at the Tasting Room. She said she was not only an accomplished violinist but also an aspiring fly fisher and wondered if I could help her along. So, when I invited her to audition her skills, she said she would love to give it a go.

We only fished one year on Christmas Day, though it was always pretty much thereabouts, sometimes as late as mid-January, as it was last year when I brought Jack. He chased some browns in the icy cold of Alder Pool as if he were still a puppy. Two weeks later, I knew there was something wrong. He was not himself, but he never complained; still young and happy, only not right. The vet said it had metastasized. I held him on my lap and rubbed his ears, told him I loved him.

From the very beginning, fishing with Kat had always been not much more than the primary excuse for lunch. In the early years, we would always pull on our waders and boots. String up our rods, tie on a small nymph 'cause trout like small flies in winter and open a bottle of wine. Kat's job is to bring her violin, a baguette, and whatever cheese she might like. The Nutshell provides all the necessities for heating the lobster bisque I have shipped in from Maine, and a cozy table to set Grandma's silver and crystal wine goblets filled with a fine French vintage.

We would fish the Swimming Hole and work our way down to the Nutshell Pool, pause for a taste of wine, and head on down to Alder Pool and beyond. One very cold and snow-covered winter day Kat spotted a snake sticking its head out of the south-facing rocks at the ancient spring. It was not a viper; white with black markings is how I remember it.

We would work our way back to the Nutshell for more wine and lunch. More often than not, Stephen and Ken, esteemed members of Friends Creek Anglers Association, would have arrived and were amused to find Kat's violin uncased laying on the bunk bed. We would share our luck and offer lunch. This happened with an astonishing degree of regularity. Uncanny.

The best fish I ever caught took a woolly bugger at the top of the Nutshell Pool. It dragged me from the top over the falls to the bottom, and he didn't stop till he was two pools down. The rainbow measured twenty inches and was fat. As the years progressed, all pretension of fishing was gone; it was all about lunch and the violin. Kat did hook some big fish now and again but broke them off. I think a knot tying lesson is in order. I caught some less impressive browns, but after fighting the big rainbow, my enthusiasm for waders and boots had waned. Fishing with Kat was all about fun.

This year would be different. I am wintering in Florida. Kat is working and going to school. Time is limited.

It will soon be spring, lots of fish are being stocked, and we are planning on returning to the original lunch menu and going back to waders, boots, fishing and the music. Maybe, hopefully, even a late spring snowstorm will provide the magic of snow on the creek.

It's good to be loved, if only a little.

FEBRUARY 27, 2014
BAY POINT
PANAMA CITY BEACH, FLORIDA

It's Thursday. The day before my stay at 408 Lagoon Towers ends. There will be only one more morning to wake up enjoying the Upper Grand Lagoon from my bedroom window; only one more morning to enjoy my morning coffee while my osprey has his morning meal. It's hard to tell a him from a her, even with binoculars.

I do not want to leave. The owner has leased it to someone else for all of March and April, starting on Saturday.

I pack my stuff. J.R. Pruitt will be here mid-afternoon to begin the process of getting me to The Orchard. Not saying "home," but I guess it is. I really do not want to leave here or go there, and not just because it's ungodly cold, snow everywhere, and Jack will not be there.

There was a time I wanted to live there. I was four, living in a row house off Erdman Avenue in Baltimore. I walked through the front door and turned left, headed to my grandparents' home in The Orchard, some forty miles to the west. Then I took another left; should've gone right. A neighbor found me on the bridge over the train tracks and returned me to the house on Emily Avenue.

I was happy to move there in 1948, even though my grandfather was no longer there. Natural causes, the only one I can recall. My grandmother could cook. My mother could not. I would not eat asparagus for nearly thirty years.

Still tethered in a highchair, she tried to make me eat limp, soggy, over-cooked, bitter asparagus before Dad could take me to the Fifth Regiment Armory for a circus to see a man shot out of a cannon. He wanted to see it more than I did. Showtime was close. He snatched me from the chair, spilling the plate of asparagus. I saw it live and again in *Octopussy*. He was probably never forgiven.

I am not at peace with leaving Bay Point and heading to The Orchard. In fact, yesterday, Jackie of Club 19 fame poured me an Amber Bock in anticipation of my usual habit of enjoying one or two with lunch. I refused it in favor of unsweetened tea. A "damn Yankee" was heard from the recesses of the kitchen. I suspect T, who makes wonderful chili and gumbo, of this slanderous outburst. I truly expect this temperate condition (the first since 1998, imposed by an outdated and rigidly enforced policy of Frederick Memorial Hospital) to end upon the arrival of J.R., who will have a stash of Jack Daniels at his son-in-law's condo on the beach, Jack Black plus Single Barrel. Under normal circumstances, J.R. and I would go to Firefly for dinner.

But today is no normal day; I'm leaving Bay Point.

Have I mentioned I don't want to go?

Club 19 has a buffet dinner once a week on Thursdays, and sometimes, the aforementioned Jackie sings and plays guitar along with her father, who she says sounds like Johnny Cash. When J.R. and I show up for dinner there are no tables left, so we sit at the bar. Jackie pours me an Amber Bock, and I introduce J.R. as the guy who is driving me home. Jackie becomes visibly upset, almost to the "here's your stinking beer, wear it" level. I had told her I was going, but she thought just for the weekend or so.

J.R. told her she was pretty. She is pretty. I like her a lot. She is the girl from the song "That's How They Do It in Dixie." Anyway, the buffet closes at seven bells, and Jackie and her dad grab their guitars. Her mother's there, too, but she doesn't sing. Jackie and her dad proceed to sing for J.R. and me; a little Dolly, some Hank the Great, and "Folsom Prison Blues," and it's all good and fun.

The place closed, but the bar was left open, and for well over an hour, it was just us. Jackie and her dad sang, and Trish poured me Amber Bock. J.R. drank Miller Lite, or was it Jack with a splash of water? Trish joined in singing, and Jackie's mother got my e-mail address, saying Jackie was going to make me a Jack Daniels Christmas bottle with lights inside it.

Just that morning, the condo owner had told me I could have the unit back this coming winter. That seemed to improve Jackie's mood. Lots of good-bye hugs all around.

It's good to be loved, if only a little.

FEBRUARY 28, 2014
BAY POINT, PANAMA CITY BEACH, FLORIDA

Osprey

I talked myself out of bed earlier than I wanted. The lagoon was as beautiful as ever under a clear sky. The blue water of the lagoon was sparkling like thousands of flickering diamonds in the sunlight. My osprey waited for me to brew my coffee before he began enjoying his fresh catch of the morning. The tide was out, and the wading birds were stalking around the edges of the marsh. Life is good — except I'm leaving Bay Point.

Eventually J.R. showed up and we began loading the Durango. The trip was planned for first heading to his home in Albany, then stopping by the Davidson River in Brevard, North Carolina, after which we'd go to Rural Retreat in Virginia for more fishing, all before eventually heading to The Orchard. Prolong the inevitable.

As we were loading up, my new Canadian friend, Larry, came by on his way to the golf course. His final admonition was to be prepared to play more golf next year. Promise to self: get my back fixed.

The drive to Albany was uneventful as best as I can remember. We did take a different route, left PCB from the west side. I don't remember why exactly, but it worked out as we got to the all-important junction of Florida Route 231 and I-10 in really good time. It usually takes an hour, and we beat that. Cotton fields were pretty much all picked clean and turned over. Pecan orchards are naturally beautiful, even in winter. There is mistletoe hanging in large clusters from the bare branches, too high to gather. All in all it was a pretty drive, if you like back-ass, two-lane Southern country roads—and I do.

It takes all of three and half hours. J.R. has plenty of stories to pass the time.

My memory is a little fuzzy on the particulars before we went to the country club for dinner. I do recall a Jack or two. There is a new chef at the Doubletree Country Club.

He came from a cruise ship line, so the buffet was really good. I had fish and white wine. The Pruitt's brought their own red. Met some new folks, and Franz and Mandy were there, whom I'd met on several previous occasions. This is the second time their daughter Shannon was out of town while I was there, and that means they stay at her plantation house and I stay at their house just two miles away. It's really a nice arrangement as Shannon's dog, Jake, requires some attention, and I really don't.

MARCH 1, 2014
ALBANY, GEORGIA

After breakfast, J.R. and I headed out for some shopping errands and to stop by the country club for Demonstration Day, where club makers show off their new drivers, mostly. I hit a Calloway and a Ping. Liked the Ping better; it was lighter. I was trying to hit the ball over a tree on the driving range, and I did. Nothing else matters. J.R. bought new golf shoes. I hope he'll play more, or at least some, this year. Because my back is so screwed up, I only played eighteen holes three times all winter. My swing is not what it once was or will be again this summer. Hope springs eternal.

J.R. had found a trap and skeet range near his house. One should always travel with a shotgun, fly rod, and a private stash, just in case. I don't remember having ever shot trap or skeet. I did have a clay pigeon throwing machine when I lived on the farm in EA. Airy, so I guess that counts, but never skeet. I'd forgotten about the machine as I loaned it to Joe Michael in 1992 and hadn't seen it since, except for once at his farm in Boonsboro fifteen years ago. Rusted.

J.R. took his very nice 28-gauge, same one he shot quail with back in November. I had my 16-gauge German side-by-side, choked rifle and full, a gift from the Widow McPherson. I hit the first one on the trap course, and it went downhill from there. Skeet was fun; did somewhat better on the crossing shots then I would have expected. Not good but better. We met a nice guy, Jimmy Harris, who sells boats. He became our trapper and tutor. J.R. needs to become a member of this club. We shot five stations of trap and eight stations of skeet for the tidy sum of $5.00 each. Hell, of a way to spend an afternoon, only to be topped off when we got back home by Jack Daniels "Sinatra" special edition; costs $150.00 a bottle. Wonderfully smooth; tastes more like a very good bourbon than sour mash. Good news is J.R. doesn't like bourbon, so it will last a while. Hitting golf balls, shooting shotguns, and drinking great whiskey all in the same day…life is good.

The Pruitts, in their well-intentioned efforts to educate my palate and make me a tad more cosmopolitan, took me to a Mexican restaurant for dinner. I had the high-grade tuna in a corn wrapper. It tasted good largely because it was cooked by an Italian chef, who was the former chef at Doubletree CC and who stopped by our table to exchange pleasantries with the Pruitts.

MARCH 2, 2014
PISGAH FOREST, NORTH CAROLINA

Julie fixed a good breakfast of eggs, bacon in the oven, and biscuits with honey. Then we packed up and headed for Brevard, North Carolina. It is a long drive. We stayed at the very private Pisgah Forest Hampton Inn. Dinner was across the parking lot in a shopping center, would you believe SARO, a Japanese restaurant in the mountains of North Carolina, and especially one where they do not twirl knives and slice mushrooms in midair. Truly excellent. I can't pronounce hibachi shrimp and chicken, but it was good.

Japanese chopsticks are round, making them very difficult to get used to. Plum wine and Japanese beer made for a great experience but did not facilitate the handling of the round chopsticks. I had my leftovers frozen and will enjoy them again in a day or so.

Kinda got off to a late start, found our way to the Davidson River Fly Shop around 10 a.m. and hired Heath to guide us for half a day. It's not so much that we could not find fishy water or know which fly to tie on without a guide; it is more that we have reached the age of enlightenment, which is not to say good sense. If either one of us were to have a difficulty, the other one would be of little or no help in getting one out of said difficulty, and we would probably both die trying. It almost happened in 2002 on the Deschutes in Oregon, steel heading, when J.R. went down. The water was chest deep and fast, filling his waders. No guide boat in sight. He was a good hundred yards upstream from me. It was impossible for me to take even one step upstream, maybe cross-current, but not upstream. We should not have been in this water. He was bobbing toward me like a cork, if I could make just one more cast. The guide showed up and plucked him from the water before I could cast him a line.

We hire guides.

J. R. found that this was Heath's real job and he was good at it, plus we learn something new from almost all guides. Heath did not have a toe ring; however, I thought he might when he said, "Set the hook downstream." The fact that he showed me how to do that proved he was not the toe ring type. And I caught fish.

It was cold, and it rained like hell. But we both caught fish, big beautiful rainbows, on dry flies in the rain, the very cold rain. There was even a snowflake or two. My legs don't work so good after several hours of standing in waist-deep, freezing cold water. Fact is, they just stopped moving altogether. It took both Heath and J.R. to get me out of the river onto the not-so-very-high riverbank.

Back in the fly shop at the end of the day, Heath even helped me pull off my boots. Don't get old.

J.R. has booked Heath for another trip in April. Heath recommended a spot for a cold beer that we could not find. But we did find the Sagebrush Steak House for some much-needed refreshment.

The Jordan Street Inn was highly recommended for dinner but was closed, so we went back to the Sagebrush Steak House largely because it was about the only place open that served adult beverages. They ran out of our favorite Tennessee whiskey pretty much just before we got there or just after we left the first time. J.R. managed one weak drink, but who can complain about steak and beer, or ribs for that matter. Fortunately, we are very well-traveled fishermen and were able to enjoy a stiff nightcap from our private supply of ardent spirits. It was a perfect ending to a great day.

Winter storm Titan canceled our trip to Rural Retreat, Virginia.

Winter storms be damned! So, I got to The Orchard two days ahead of schedule.

Oh, Happy Day.

THE ORCHARD

As America's frontiersmen began to push westward, The Orchard became a recognized geographical area around 1764. Structures began to be erected along the only road. It runs for a little over a half mile east to west, known as the National Pike. The turn of the next century brought brick sidewalks. Maple trees lined both sides of the road, forming a canopy and providing shade. Things moved slowly back then, must be something in the water, as things still move slow. It was located at the forks of the main road from Baltimore to Hagerstown and the Buffalo Road a major north-south route. The Buffalo Road is now extinct as is any semblance of anything interesting to do since the War Between the States.

JUNE 28, 1863
THE ORCHARD
THE HILLS HAVE NAMES

Local legend has it that General Winfield S. Hancock chose to bivouac some of his troops at Love Spring on Cool Spring Farm a short distance northeast of town, fresh water being the necessity.

Under orders from General George G. Meade, Hancock had marched his troops under a boiling hot sun the thirty-two miles from Monocacy Junction, near Frederick, to The Orchard. Winfield commanded the II Corps, Army of the Potomac.

He marched up Bark Hill to enter the town from the west. Had he turned onto the first road on the left, upon entering town, he would have gone up and down Lazy Hill. On a clear day he could have seen Big Round Top from the cemetery that rests on the crest of Lazy Hill. Upon entering the town, a Yankee soldier in his company observed that it was a pretty secluded village, patriotic, but paralyzed just now by the nearness of the rebel army.

Hancock was looking for Lee's Army of Northern Virginia. Instead, he damn near found J. E. B. Stuart and three brigades of his Confederate cavalry. The Orchard's townsfolk warned him Stuart was camped seven miles away in Westminster. General Hancock chose not to act on this local intelligence and did not launch what might have been a surprise attack. Had he heeded this information and headed east to Westminster he would have gone down Meadow Branch Hill and changed history in the process.

When growing up here, Cool Spring Farm was one of my favorite places to roam around with my black and white English springer spaniel, Jinx. Even if I had a dog, I could not do it now.

JUNE 28, 2016
THE ORCHARD

The village is still secluded and patriotic. The Orchard is nestled into the green rolling hills of Carroll County, Maryland. The purple hue of the Blue Ridge Mountains forms a beautiful backdrop on the western horizon. The stars and stripes fly from the front porches of many of the homes, and not just on holidays. A closer look and you will see the stars and bars on the back porch. The Segafoose Hotel where Hancock and his officers took their comfort is now a private residence with a historical marker in the front yard. Love Spring is still there, I reckon, but there are lots of locked gates and barbed wire fences keeping the corn from fraternizing with the soybeans that keep me from exploring. Where dairy farms used to be have now become chopped up horse pastures. Holding pens are now front yards.

The Rising Sun Tavern closed in 1842. That same year the Crossed Keys Tavern also closed, leaving only the Segafoose Hotel, which had gained and maintained a grand reputation for food and entertainment.

My house was built in 1842. The timing is ironic, as my back porch has developed a grand reputation for fine food, wine, entertainment, and very good American whiskey. Maintaining The Orchard's long-lost tradition for fine food and drink is just about the only reason I can think of for living here.

The Orchard's heyday came to an end around 1885. The town had almost died. The clockmaker, silversmith, hatter, cigar maker, several cabinet makers, haberdasher, and the tannery had shut down. All were gone. It was no longer the main thoroughfare from Baltimore to Pittsburgh. The railroad chose a different direction. There remained three stores, three churches, and one bank to serve the four hundred residents. Things stayed pretty much stayed the same for eighty years. Most folks kept chickens, and some fed them table scraps. Vegetable gardens and out-houses are few and far between. Farm animals are no longer kept in back yards. The nearest respectable golf course is thirty miles away and expensive.

In the 1970s, things started to change again. The two stores that sold gasoline closed. The one that survived housed the post office in a front corner. At that time each house had its own post office box. The store was not self-service. Penny candy, cigarettes, dry goods, assorted meats, gossip, and the world's most delicious ice cream were there to meet every need. The last was made in an outbuilding behind the store with the cream of local Holsteins -- unregulated, uncertified, and not homogenized. The store was the gathering place. A sign still hangs there today declaring it to be Devilbiss's Store. Everybody just called it Mr. Tom's. The Great Fire of 1976 reduced one church and several houses to ashes. The bank got bought by a bigger bank and closed. Today, all the stores are gone.

I could have most probably enjoyed living here in The Orchard's golden years, except for the lack of indoor plumbing.

Given my age and the maladies inflected by the wages of sin, I will spend the summer tending my roses, praying for deliverance.

NOVEMBER 30, 2014
PRAYERS ANSWERED
ROAD TRIP 2014

Arrived home to The Orchard last evening after eighteen days on the road. Much like this past March, I did not want to leave where I was and come here...almost. There are four or five routes to get from Albany to

The Orchard, and they all take fourteen plus hours. Some might think that the least likely one of those goes through Orangeburg.

Had I not recently spent three weeks in Orangeburg, I would have chosen a different route. It is all pretty much back-ass country roads for about five hours, where you drove for miles and miles without seeing another car. Just loved it.

I stopped first at Duke's ABC; my new friend O'burg Junior. and his family own the store. Junior was not there; seems he is still celebrating Thanksgiving. I picked up another bottle of Blanton's. Next stop, the House of Pizza to see Miss Savannah, who owns the place with her brother, but he does not work there. She does part-time when she is not working for the school district. She was surprised and happy to see me again. Then on to the Jay-Birds bar. The owner is a slight man, small of stature, thinning black-gray hair with a sharp, straight nose on an angular face. He scurries around behind the bar like the small brown birds that flit amongst the bushes along the banks of rivers and streams.

Thomas Braxton Bryant IV showed up and settled the five-dollar wager he lost a month ago by buying drinks for most of the rest of the night, which takes us to the Black River Tavern, also owned by Miss Savannah and her brother. Junior tracks me down and brings along Peggy Sue, his new girlfriend, saying they are going to get married. I'm invited to the wedding. Should children result from this union, they will grow up to play linebacker at Clemson University. Fell in love in the three weeks that I was gone, imagine that. We all ended up at The Bank Social Club, by any measure a dive. The air is blue with smoke, and some of it smells funny. They do not have a closing time, and it's the only place in the county open for booze on Sunday. Membership is required but is automatic when you show up with Junior and Tom. There is a DJ. The four pool tables had been rearranged to allow for a small dance floor. The blonde at the bar could twirl but would not slow dance. Ginger was her name. I told Tom to put his stupid knife away. He did, and I needed to go home.

The closer I got, the more I tried to find a reason to postpone getting there. I am still unsuccessful at making The Orchard feel like home without Jack.

One reason, most likely, is I've only been in The Orchard ten days since the first week in September. My fee assignment with the South Carolina school system was for seven weeks: three in Columbia and three in Orangeburg, best three in a long time, and one good week in Greenville. Again, I did not want to go back to The Orchard when that assignment was over.

It had snowed in Greenville, and the mountains of Brevard were not fit to fish, so we decided to check out the beach instead, which was too cold. No luck in hooking up in Charleston, so I headed north.

I had met Miss O'Malley very briefly last April and have had no contact since then. She qualifies as age appropriate by the Hemingway standard and is very easy on the eyes, smart, and a world traveler. I reached out to her on the drive home. We spent seven hours, twenty-three minutes together during the ten days I was home. We had dinner twice, which was more than exceptionally special and magical. Bang-shang-a-lang-bang-bang goes my heart.

I am beginning to wonder why I don't want to be here. The Orchard is still a pretty town. It is not the same as I left it forty-seven years ago. The Orchard has not grown any, still it is not as I remember. A long-time resident says, "It is all dressed up with no place to go." The Sons of Temperance disbanded in 1883 and no new taverns have opened in the ensuing hundred and some odd years. Beginning as early as 1911, some of the brick sidewalks were replaced with concrete. A politician moved to town, thought the road needed improvement. It was widened enough to cover the feeder roots of the maple trees and has a double yellow line down its middle. The maple leaf canopy is now gone, but we have a wide road with a double yellow line down its middle.

From the time I was old enough to draw a bow, about seven or eight years before passing my driver's exam on the second try, I roamed the fields and woodlands with a quiver of homemade arrows slung over my back and a straight hickory bow pretty near every day. Jinx, a black and white Springer Spaniel, field bred, with a twenty-yard nose, was my constant and only companion, always anxious for me to get home from school.

He ran free ahead of me.

There were bobwhite quail then; he knew their call. There were wild pheasants then, too. I missed a lot of flushes. Back before crop rotation became popular, there was a corn field at the corner of Trevanion Rd and Baust Church Rd. During harvest the stalks were cut and chocked leaving rows for foot high stubble. Jinx would hunt the chocked corn, running as fast as he could from one to another. One fine day he jerked himself to the right and flushed a cock bird form a row of stubble. I was not even close enough o get a shot off but I did and missed and lost the arrow. I think he knew I could not hit a flushed bird with an arrow; the bird was too fast and the bow too slow. The nest year in the same field he went straight away for the spot he had flushed the pheasant the year before. The bird was not there. He never quit.

There were few deer then, only in the mountains. It was early fall once when he and I were headed home near dark in what had been a hay field just north of town. It was close enough to the house to hear my father whistling, beckoning us to dinner. A big buck and two does bolted out of Devilbiss's wood, over the open field, toward the woods behind Clear Spring Farm. Jinx gave a short chase.

After supper, I scampered as only a ten-year-old can do down to Mr. Tom's, where the old people would be gossiping, and enjoying the most delicious ice cream in the world. I excitedly reported the extraordinary deer sighting because deer were rare and hunting season was near.

"Don't come in here tellin' lies, kid."

Everyone knew deer were only in the mountains. Nobody else had a bird dog, not even a respectable hound. Ill will abounds, contempt, maybe just jealousy. I had never milked a cow or made hay. Fisher did, lost his right leg in a thrashing machine.

Jinx could be a rabbit dog. He scared up one in a chopped and shocked corn field with knee-high stubble. He turned it back toward me, full speed, ten rows over. I knew it was a kill before I released the arrow. I still get that same sensation every time it's a kill shot. It took him a couple or three tries to figure out how not to stick himself with the arrow, but he brought it to hand. Mother would not cook or eat it, but the neighbor who kept pigeons would.

At Mr. Tom's that evening, some old man remarked, "Heard you killed a rabbit."

"Yeah," I smiled.

"Must have been a sick or stupid rabbit," snarled some old woman.

Elbows jabbed ribs, backs got slapped, funniest thing the old gossipers ever heard. Nobody ever shot a bow or had a bird dog.

I had never milked a cow or made hay. But I have since sailed up the Nile and pared the Road Hole.

NOVEMBER 14, 2014
HELEN, NORTH GEORGIA
ON THE ROAD AGAIN

Somewhere along the way between Ashville and Helen I stopped for breakfast at Henry's Restaurant, but lunch was all there was. Fried chicken, mashed potatoes with brown gravy, greens, and cobbler for dessert, all home cooked. It wasn't Henry, the person who welcomed me, but he ran the place, tipped in at about five hundred and some odd pounds, seated behind a plate piled high with fried chicken topped with breaded pork chops, and I couldn't see what was under that. It was 10:30 in the morning. After determining I was by myself, he invited me to join him at the family table. I chose a seat two down from him, no need to rub elbows. Ten dollars flat for all you could eat. When he discovered I was just passing through, conversation became Southern polite. I limited myself to one helping and sweet tea.

It only took a couple of hours to drive from Ashville to Helen. I don't remember where I met J. R. Pruitt before we checked into our condo's courtesy of his son-in-law, Doctor Grant. We each had our own. I arrived there several hours before J.R. did. He showed up just about happy hour. A couple of proper whiskeys later, we headed out for dinner.

Red wine was ordered to complement a rib eye at Paul's, "The best steak in town," on the river, served in the bar by the comely Amanda, smoking permitted.

I would not be drawn into a discussion about what would be good for the country.

Suddenly and unexpectedly, there appeared a three-piece country band, followed in short order by a procession of ten lovely ladies, out-of-towners, for a night on the town. J.R. declared we had died and gone to heaven. Drinking red wine or drinking wine of any type in a honky tonk reflects poorly on one's manhood and is just wrong, to some sacrilegious, and to others, dangerous. J.R. matched my wine with Miller Lite, one for one, also just wrong. I hoped the ten lovely ladies would not notice.

The band was playing a classic slow country song, and the ladies had been served their first round. Approaching the head of their table, arms extended and palms up, I asked, "Ladies, who's first?" The ice was broken; as the evening wore on it melted. J.R didn't dance a lot, spent most of the time spinning yarns with charm, wit, and personality; developed some lasting relationships. I concentrated on Sally Ann, apparently the leader of the group. Danced almost every dance with her and all that required being held close. We were both in love for a time.

Having been married for more years than I care to remember, I have missed out on a lot of lot hunting and fishing, and now I have found a honky-tonk bar. There is almost nothing more inspiring and invigorating, and nothing that will induce a total loss of self-awareness, than holding a beautiful women for several hours, a bit more hooch than you need, and a hundred or so drunk red-necks singing at the top of their voices. The band brought the house and me down with a raucous rendition of David Allen Coe's "The Perfect Country Song." The perfect song to end a honk-tonk night. J.R. remembered I had told him I had to go home somewhere after eleven drinks and o'clock. Apparently, I was buying dinner, wine, beers, and a round for the ladies. The comely Amanda forgot some.

It does not matter if we fished Smith Creek on Saturday or Sunday. The weather was damn cold and wet. We had fished Smith Creek several years ago. On that trip we stayed in the cabins in the state park and I proudly brought a bottle of Midleton's Irish Whiskey, which I had bought in the Dublin airport, paying nine-ninety dollars. It is rare and very good. J.R. would have none of it, not a wee dram. Got right shitty about it, so I enjoyed it all by myself. This was also the trip J.R. lost his "beaver stick" from Maine. I will not get into the water without mine, even though the Smith is not much of a river. At least it isn't where we fish it, more a creek than river. We were led to believe the creek had been stocked with 1,200 rainbows two weeks ago. They were not to be found, but we did not walk up to the dam, where the water was deeper and colder. The Smith River skunked us on both trips. J.R. could barely walk back to the car. It was my first real reason for concern. This was not a structural problem; it was an organic problem. Something inside him was not working like it should.

Helen bills itself as an Alpine village and offers a good selection of German food, architecture, and all things Alpine. After a very good traditional dinner at what looked from the outside as if it served proper German food, and it did, we headed back to Paul's. The same band was already into their first set. The ten lovely ladies from Thomaston had saved two places at their table for us. Sally Ann and I danced together again most of the night. I told her I really liked our last dance last night, she said she did too. That was about all we said to each other in two nights. For an all-too-brief time, we were in a different world, our bodies melting together, fused by the rhythm of that slow country song like never, ever. We were one. Please band, keep on playing.

The beds in our condo had mirrors at the headboard. Under certain circumstances, this could be fun, but not if the first thing you see after a night at a honky tonk is your own self.

Clear the gauzy haze from between your ears.

I'm pretty sure it was Saturday when we needed something from Walmart in Cleveland, stuff for the new GoPro and a cable to make my iPod work in the truck. It is only seven miles from Helen, yet somehow, on the way back, after about thirty minutes, we saw a road sign that said twelve miles to Murphy, N.C. The Chattahoochee National Forest is very beautiful, and sometimes you can't get from where you are to where you want to go.

NOVEMBER 18, 2014
SOMEWHERE NEAR BLUE RIDGE, NORTH GEORGIA
STILL DAMN COLD

J.R. booked a half-day of quail hunting. More reason for concern. Never mind that the route he chose to get to Noontootla Creek Farms was one switchback after another. It took forever.

Don't remember the guide's name, but his Brittany's name was Belle. In short order, Miss Belle came to point. The covey was flushed. Two shots rang out and Belle was on retrieve for the dead birds. J.R. had just stopped, as if on his own point, and stood there frozen in place, without shouldering his gun. He assured me he was not having a heart attack, while he was standing there looking for all the world as if he were having one. I offered to put an end to his suffering. Belle brought two quail to hand. The guide and I gave J.R. a helping hand back to the club house and a better route back to Helen. I had to drive.

We got back to Helen in time for happy hour at Mully's Nocoochee Grill, across the road from the Unicoi Fly Shop. The place was packed, so we took a seat at the bar for a few whiskeys before dinner. The staff became overwhelmed by the overflow crowd and called in Mully for help, who joined us at the bar. Mully is the former mayor of Helen and pretty much rules this part of the world. Dinner was excellent, and Mully poured some local wine that was also surprisingly good as he told very good stories. Promised J.R. he could get him on some prized private trout water. I reminded them both that my Georgia license is good for a year.

The next morning, I had a tough love talk with J.R. I even said I'd quit drinking with him, knowing full well I still had ten days to go. He declined.

NOVEMBER 19, 2014
EDISTO SPORTING CLUB, NORTH GEORGIA
WARMED UP SOME

J.R. had invited his grand-nephew Nick to join us for a couple of days. He, too, has his own condo, which turned out to be good because his wife showed up with their sixteen-month-old daughter. We met Nick at the Edisto Sporting Clay's course for a fifty-target warm-up to an afternoon hunt. Nick is a Presbyterian minister in Atlanta, as is his wife. We did not distinguish ourselves at sporting clays. I tried shooting my 16-gauge, but it needed some oil to get it open, then it really did not like the high brass seven and a half shells and refused to close. So J.R. shared his 12-gauge, and that did not fit very well, but it was all good and fun. Nick shot a 12-gauge automatic pretty well, but he had never been on a bird hunt. It is a little too much gun for a quail hunt.

After sporting clays, we met our guide, a Baptist preacher; don't know his name, just called him Preacher. He took us for lunch at Pit Stop, which advertised itself as not a fast-food restaurant. Preacher could spin a yarn and kept us amused until our good, slow-cooked food arrived. Preacher asked Nick to say the blessing, and he obliged.

Preacher had three Brittany Spaniels. All were pretty good but not as good as Preacher had advertised at lunch. He carried a snake stick to prod the pointed birds into flight. "Yes, it's a snake stick; the only ones I've seen out here were dead." These were not wild birds or even hold-over birds, but they were still fun. Twenty-four were put out. We harvested sixteen plus three chuckers. Nick made some long shots with his 12-gauge, prompting Preacher to ask if he became a Presbyterian, would he shoot like that.

The shooting field was grass rows separated by rows of sorghum or sugarcane, depending what part of the country you are from. The grass fields were peppered with holes caused by rotting tree roots. The holes are about the size of a groundhog hole and go straight down. The grass had grown over them, so you could not see them. The first one I stepped in just caused a minor stumble. Being in the presence of two men of the cloth, my oath was pretty mild.

Preacher noticed J.R. had stopped walking and got on his phone and ordered him a mule to ride him around the fields. Both Nick and I were a bit surprised when an ATV showed up. We were sure Preacher meant the four-legged kind. J. R. shot the rest of the day from a seated position.

Preacher's dog, Lady, and his other young dog were on at the edge of the grass, pointing into the sorghum. Preacher was to my right, more in front than he should have been, and Nick was to his right at three o'clock. As Preacher flushed the birds, they took off straight out in front of him. I brought my gun up, flipped off the safety, stepped into the shot, and my left leg went straight down up to the hip. I knew two things in less than a heartbeat: My leg was about to break, and I was about to shoot Preacher. The mind puts everything into slow motion. The barrels swung past Preachers' head; I got my hand around the trigger guard and prayed don't drop it, laying the gun gently and quietly on the grass. The leg didn't break. Preacher asked if I was okay. I said "No" because I wasn't sure yet. Once I took inventory and found no pain, I worried about whose hole I had fallen into. I had not found the bottom. Preacher pulled me out quickly. J.R. and Nick each brought down a bird.

Preacher spun another yarn about an old bird dog of his, now gone. Sunglasses help disguise it but shooting quail through tears is just wrong. The temperature dropped. We were all tired and had about an hour of daylight left, so called it a day.

NOVEMBER 20, 2014
FERN VALLEY, SOQUE RIVER,
CLARKSVILLE, NORTH GEORGIA
NICE DAY

J.R. had prepared a pork loin for dinner. He is a damn good cook. He put it in a 125-degree oven before we left for Fern Valley, which is owned by Glad and Marty Simmons. This is private water at its finest. Water was gin clear. Big rainbows, bigger browns, and the flow was perfect for wading. Fish were lined up on the near bank, making it necessary to wade in downstream to the far bank and circle upstream to present a nymph down in the current. J.R. and I shared the first pool about twenty yards apart. Pretty damn quick, a huge rainbow took J.R.'s woolly bugger. Biggest rflyainbow he ever caught rivaled the one I caught in Alaska. I tried to get over to him to help with the net and get a photo but was too slow. No photo, but I saw the fish, at least twenty-six inches.

J.R. moved upstream. I fished the pool for some time without luck and lost contact with J.R. Later, we agreed to carry radios from then on. I scouted the lower part of the river from a high bank for about a half mile, came across a pod of about a dozen feeding on the surface. The nymph would not work so replaced it with a dry stimulator, #14 white with a yellow parachute, waded in downstream, and stepped in a chest-deep hole. Slow going; it took a long time to get into position. I was thirty feet upstream in knee-high water; drifted the fly over the pod, and a nice rainbow was fooled. My waders were leaking and both feet soaking wet and heavy; water was forty-four degrees. Every proper presentation brought another and bigger rainbow to the net. The fifth and last was a twenty-four inch plus brown in full colors; broke off the fly in my net. I was trembling cold and could not tie on another. I had a long and difficult wade to the bank, a more difficult climb up the bank to the trail back to the sixty some odd stairs that led up to the house; a long way with cold, heavy feet.

I reached the house just as Glad was returning from a shopping trip. I complimented her scarf and told her she looked natty, asked her to help me out of my boots. She did and pulled off my waders. She put my socks and wading fleece in the dryer, and her husband, Marty, went down to the river to find J.R. and Nick to let them know I was in the house.

Nick was not having a good day. J.R. and Nick fished for another couple of hours as I recovered under the care of Glad. Hot chocolate felt good. The sweet smell of chicken and dumplin's spilled from the kitchen. We talked a lot about life, kindness, as two old dogs lay nearby. She twirled her hair.

Nick's wife, Mia, and their child arrived for dinner. J.R.'s pork loin was cooked to perfection. Mia provided the blessing. From somewhere a bottle of Single Barrel Jack appeared and was very much enjoyed. Mia found wine to her liking. I think the baby drank milk but cannot swear to it. Presbyterian ministers are quite libertarian, some say free thinkers. Nick is a nice guy, and Mia is very charming.

Over after-dinner drinks, J.R. brought up our experience at Paul's the past weekend. He allowed how if I cleaned it up, I could relate my experience with the lovely lady from Thomaston; must have been concerned for the baby's tender ears. I just said it was the best sex ever on a dance floor, and it was. The only time that came even close was as a senior in high school when I slow danced at a sock hop in the gym with my French teacher.

NOVEMBER 21, 2014
HELEN TO ALBANY, GEORGIA
NICE CLEAR DAY

It's a five-hour drive to Albany. We decide it would be best to meet at Salt Lick in Cordele, as GPS doesn't really know the best way to Albany. Somewhere north of Atlanta I decided to ask Miss O'Malley to marry me. Somewhere south of Atlanta I thought better of it; must have been white-line fever. I got to the Salt Lick about twenty minutes ahead of J.R.; had a beer and chips while I waited. Then off we went to his house, where J.R.'s wife Julie welcomed me with open arms, really nice to see her again. I told her I was worried about J.R., and she said she was, too, that she might retire to take care of him. A short nap, then off to the country club for dinner with J.R.'s daughter Shannon and her husband, Grant, who was coming down with the flu. There was another new chef. We couldn't thank Grant enough for his generosity in providing the condos.

It's good to love and be loved.

NOVEMBER 22, 2014
ALBANY TO THOMASVILLE, GEORGIA, TO PCB
RAIN IN FORECAST

Plantation Days in Thomasville is much like the Waterfowl Festival on Maryland's Eastern Shore -- all about quail, pointers, and setters, shotguns and fly fishing. Stopped by Kevin's Emporium to replace two broken wine glasses. They were out of the quail white wine glasses, so I replaced it with a pheasant design, like the red wine, which was also replaced. Wonderful antique store down the street reminded me I have some A. B. Frost prints somewhere. Locals suggested Jimmy's Shrimp and Grits for lunch, but it was too crowded. Found Gin River Plantation Restaurant around the corner only because J.R. had to go and could not wait; it turned out to be a treasure. Best Brunswick stew ever. Tasted local Georgia wines; two were drinkable, and two were too sweet.

It started to rain, so we headed to Panama City Beach to stay in Grant and Shannon's condo on the beach. J.R. wanted to have dinner at Dee's. We usually eat at Firefly. I was driving; therefore, my choice prevailed, and we got there just in time for the early bird special. Still expensive, but worth it. I bought. Not much to do but watch football.

Sunday neither of us wanted to go out for breakfast, so for lunch we checked to see if the Club 19 was open at Bay Point. I doubted it would be because they usually do not open if there are no golfers, and there would not be any that day; rain and more rain. Wrong. There'd been an ownership change. Gary was still manager, though. We got caught up with him, the new changes, and Jackie. Food was good and not expensive, so we went back for dinner. Jackie was supposed to work, or so we were told, but she did not. I left her a note.

We left PCB on Monday, in the rain, and headed to Tallahassee to pick up some seafood to hold us over until the turkey was served. The road back to Albany is lined with longleaf pines and live oaks. The land is soft and gentle, like an ole sweet song; cotton fields were pretty much all picked but not yet turned over. Pecan orchards are beautiful in winter, like a chorus of gangly ballerinas pirouetting. All in all, a pretty drive, if you like back-ass two-lane Southern country roads—and I do. Takes about one and half hours. J.R. has plenty of stories so it doesn't take that long, and he is still fiddling with my iPod.

THANKSGIVING DAY, 2014
ALBANY, GEORGIA
A NICE DAY

The whole point of the last fifteen days was to get to this day. Grant is sick, so dinner will not be at Shannon's plantation house. Franz and Mandy show up at the Pruitt's about five thirty. They were surprised and seemed pleased to once again find me there. Shannon got there around four, and the wine began to flow. Merry Edwards is now my favorite Sauvignon Blanc. Mandy is in rare form, funny, charming, inquisitive, and provocative. Franz has been fishing in Panama and says it's the best place in the world but will not reveal the price tag. The "Willy" bird was cooked to perfection, along with the all the accompaniments. J.R. is a damn good cook.

Julie said the blessing with a bit of a tear in her eye.

DECEMBER 7, 2014
THE ORCHARD, MARYLAND
A DAY OF INFAMY

The Widow McPherson invited me to dinner for my birthday. I had not heard from her in six months and was happy to accept. We had dated very regularly for several years. My travels had taken a toll; put a chill on the relationship, and the fact that she would not leave her cats to accompany me didn't help any.

Her farm is about twenty minutes from The Orchard. I was running late, sober, but twenty miles an hour over the limit. The sheriff, parked by the side of the Mt. Union Lutheran Church, turned his red and blue flashers on before I even got to him. I pulled the Range Rover right up next to him, so he would not have to walk so far.

"Mr. West, you in a hurry?"

"Yes, sir. I have a date, and I am late."

"This won't take long," he promised.

"Not to worry, Officer. I'm not going to get laid anyway."

He came back with a warning ticket and wished me better luck.

He was a different sheriff. I am fortunate he was not one of the other four who also objected to my penchant for speed. All were on a Friday night, all under the influence, and all at Mt. Union Lutheran Church. It takes a while to adjust your behavior when you have spent years walking home from happy hour to having to drive twenty-five miles from The Tasting Room to The Orchard.

For the four that counted, my lawyer had me dress in Brooks Brother's gray with a white shirt and blue tie and be sincere. His opening statement: "Look at him, Your Honor; he's old."

JANUARY 24, 2015
CHRISTMAS WITH KAT
A FRIENDS CREEK TRADITION RESUMED

"If the sun don't come up tomorrow, people, I've had a good time." Hank Williams, Jr., "Country State of Mind," 2003.

A tradition disrupted is all the sweeter upon resumption. The past eighteen months have been some of the very best of my entire life, perhaps more than just some, which only proves the adage that you need not have money to have a life well lived. At times, some money would have been a good thing, and at times I did have some, but having some or not having some did not contribute to this declaration. Wonderful friends, new and old, exciting new places and adventures, promising new traditions, continuing established ones, and resuming disrupted ones are all the basis of the good.

We missed our tradition last year, school and travel got in the way. But this year, Kat and I are taking a picnic to Friends Creek. Kat is no longer going to school or working this month. The Tasting Room is closed for renovations, which is having reverse effects on our respective financial conditions. I am living in The Orchard, and I would rather not be here, but have no place else to go.

I have only been here six weeks or so since the end of August. Having worked in some face time with Miss O'Malley, I feel like a cat chasing its tail. A birthday dinner with the Widow McPherson, an international New Year's Skype with Ph.D. Penelope cooking lentils, and a goose hunt with Mike and his son Will over on the Eastern Shore, plus a formal candlelight dinner with Martin and two of his lady friends, grilled venison in my dining room, along with a roaring fire in the kitchen fireplace.

Discovering the late-blooming wildflowers on the banks of the Soque River may prove to be one of the most rewarding happenings of my life. Having a true family relationship with my Pennsylvania cousins has already proven to be a significant enlargement of my life.

And now Kat. Friends Creek is truly magical in the snow, and we just had a good snow three days ago and again last night. It is a lovely setting for good food and wine and some good-sized trout. Kat and I have been at this for more years then I remember. Maybe ten or so. Each year proves to be more special the older I get.

The menu has been set lobster risotto. I made the oyster stew this morning, and there'll be whatever bread and cheese Kat brings. I am sometimes tempted to bring along a mason jar of the finest corn whiskey ever made, but at 190 proof, it will make your clothes fall off, and could have an adverse effect on tying on a fly and make the road home a little harder to stay on, to say nothing of one's situational judgment. We will settle for very good wine. Cigars? We are ever vigilant for Stephen and Ken.

Hunting Creek Outfitters has returned my waders to Orvis to either repair or replace because of the leaks suffered on the Soque at Fern Valley. I have my wellies. It is cold, and worse, windy. She has lost her reel, but no worries; I have a spare. It might be the same place as my deck shoes, which have not been seen since she and I fished Friends Creek several years ago. Must have been the year I did not forget to bring the best corn whiskey ever. Kat remembers it was three bottles of wine, white lightning, and cigars.

There is no recollection of fishing.

I was here just before Christmas with Miss O'Malley. I felt guilty. The winter here is our place, mine and Kat's. Could not find a fish then; must have been providence. The owner said there were some rainbows holding by the rock in Hogan's Pool, but he had not caught one in over a month. Maybe they too knew it was wrong.

Today, however, is different. I forgot the risotto, despite waking up in the middle of the night to take it out of the freezer. Also left the cigars at home, which is most likely for the best. Kat forgot her waders but brought several kinds of wonderful cheese and some kind of cranberry spread that was terrific. The snow last night was one of those wet, slushy kind and stuck to everything. The woods and creek were spectacularly beautiful. I forgot my camera, but Kat has an iPhone, so it doesn't matter. The Nutshell door will not unlock, but I got the padlock off. The blade of a Swiss Army Knife serves as the key for the sliding door. Resorted to the vernacular, it opened.

The deck overlooks the Nutshell Pool from about fifteen feet above. Opened a pinot noir. The Pool was alive with rising trout, gulping, flashing, breaking the surface. Ravenous and aggressive, must have been a dozen or more, a hatch of some kind. High and fast water had submerged the Kilimanjaro rock. String up our rods, tie on a dry? Or drink our wine and just watch? It was a bit too windy in the wrong direction, and we were too far away to identify the hatch, plus the snow was unspoiled. The wine was good.

Kat uncased her violin. I shadow danced to a Strauss waltz, with a flourish I twirled and dipped my bamboo rod.

Hiked to the end of the property, Hogan's Pool. Strange tracks in the snow, fresh deer tracks, raccoon prints, but some were not so easy, cat maybe. I need my beaver stick to stay upright on the icy trail. Kat is nimbler and declines a folding walking stick. Ice covered with snow makes it difficult to know what's underneath, stream or trail. Kat almost found out. It is a long walk, slipping and sliding up and down icy hills, slippery rocks hiding under the snow, climbing over and ducking under fallen trees. It can work up an appetite.

Time stands still. We open the doors. The water splashes over the rocks becoming quiet in the deep pool. White wine with oyster stew, a tradition resumed. I love her. We love each other.

It is good to love and be loved.

FEBRUARY 3, 2015
QUEPOS, COSTA RICA
ESTOY CANSADO Y DORORIDO – BILLFISH ON THE FLY
PUERTO QUEPOS

The boat is circling at trolling speed about twenty miles offshore. The Pacific is deep blue and peaceful. We are in search of sailfish on the fly. The twenty-seven-foot center console panga has plastic teasers trailing from its two outriggers. Two other rods are in their holders over the wheelhouse. They are trailing more colorful teasers behind the boat inside the outrigger's teasers. Two more rods are trailing ten-inch live Ballyhoo directly behind the boat, without hooks.

Suddenly, a fin breaks the surface; the mate and captain grab the live bait rods and begin to reel in like crazy. The big fish has attacked one of the live bait and now is chasing the other. The mate reels as fast as he can, keeping the Ballyhoo just out of reach of the hungry fish. The sailfish is getting closer and closer to the boat. When he is within ten yards, the mate yanks the hook less bait out of the water.

The fly rod is in my right hand, a pink and white fly held carefully in my left, thirty feet of line curls at my bare feet. Watch your toes. Stay off it. Roll cast shoot the line, the fly is yanked from my fingers and lands slightly behind the fish to the outside, keep the rod tip low. The frenzied fish sees the fly. He turns, hold the line tight, and *bam*. He sets the hook himself. Hold on. The jumping begins, he tail walks for what seems like forever.

The reel sings, the line is gone; only backing now. The struggle is fierce. I have no fighting seat. A rod holder is velcroed around my waist. Hold on, no shoes. The monster fish jumps time and again, with the mate yelling "Reel, reel, reel faster, reel." The boat does not back into the fight; it is all angler and fish, the way it should…

Bang, bang, bang

Something is wrong.

"Wake up, the taxi is here," J. R. Pruitt yelled through the closed window while banging loudly on the hotel room door.

"Huh, what? All right, all right. What taxi?" I garbled.

"The one to take us to the boat," he yelled.

Damn, I'm tired. The sun is not yet up, but I am now, damn.

The hotel night shift had made coffee. There was no breakfast.

FEBRUARY 1, 2015
SAN JOSE, COSTA RICA

J.R. and I consider ourselves fly fisherman. I must muster up a modicum of modesty here. I'm not a great or even good one, but yes, I am a fly fisherman, and certainly J.R. Pruitt is one. Fly fisherman keep a bucket list. Catching a billfish on a fly is a must on the list, even if they do it just once.

We flew into San Jose on Friday afternoon. Our first steps in Costa Rica were into a gleaming polished steel and glass modern airport. We were whisked through Customs and Immigration in the diplomatic queue by a representative of the tour company J.R. used to book this trip.

The plan called for spending the night there and heading out to

Quepos tomorrow. San Jose is world-renowned for maybe one thing: Hotel Del Rey. It is more known as a casino and a place to meet world-class ladies of the evening—chicca. We did not darken its door, due to jet lag or age. We stayed at the Park Hotel. It is a new, eco-friendly facility, whose energy efficiency and technology proved a challenge, a cool place.

We found our way to La Muni via recommendation, two blocks toward the cemetery and a half block left, for lunch. La Muni is a local café where we met Oscar, who interpreted our wishes for a local beer and red beans and rice to the lovely and friendly Roxanne. She had no knowledge of Americano and came out with a giant chicken leg and fried plantains. Delicious. Oscar is of German descent; his family arrived in Costa Rica 150 years ago, or maybe shortly before the end of World War II.

We went back for dinner, or Roxanne. We would not walk in this neighborhood if we were in Washington or Baltimore, but we felt safe enough. The architecture is jerry-rigged; everything seems undone. Construction has either just begun or never finished, and the area had fallen into decay. Iron gates and padlocks secured doors, a chain-linked fence topped with bales of razor wire pretty much protected everything on both sides of the street, every business, every street, every highway, everywhere from the airport to the hotel to La Muni. Crime cannot possibly be a problem. La Muni was packed with locals, all friendly. Roxanne did not get off work until eleven, way too late.

We were about five or six blocks from "downtown" and decided to take a cab to Max's American Bar, the opposite direction from downtown and the Hotel Del Rey. We did some shots and beer at the upstairs bar with some local folks of a younger generation. J.R. might remember what the shot was, all I know is it was Tums hot. Fodor's says this is a good night spot, must be a late-night spot. I was tired, there were no lovely ladies, and it was time for me to retire for the evening. It was still light out.

NOTE TO SELF: If I do this again, and I very well might, plan to arrive in San Jose on a Thursday. Gather enough rest to visit the Hotel Del Rey on Friday night. Dress properly, have lots of cash. There is no hurry to get anywhere else on Saturday or even Sunday for that matter. Pura Vida.

FEBRUARY 3, 2015
FALLS RESORT HOTEL, MANUAL ANTONIO NATIONAL PARK

From the window of the taxi, San Jose is looking prosperous this morning. There are beautiful parks, football fields, and lots of people enjoying themselves. This is a very different impression from yesterday. Seems everyone from the Central Valley heads to the Pacific Coast beaches on the weekend.

Jose, our van driver, picked us up early for the lovely four-hour drive to Quepos. There is a stop at the Croc River, which at first glance appears to be a tourist trap. We enjoy a refreshing loco coco and photograph crocs in the river. I suspect all taxi drivers have a commission arrangement with the loco coco vendors. The road winds its way through dry hills to lush mountain rainforests and into miles and miles of palm tree plantations. It is the palm oil capital of the world; once banana plantations, now palm oil. The bananas moved to the Caribbean side.

The small villages along the way are all brightly painted in varying shades of yellow, green, or blue, with an occasional red mixed in for drama. The overhead utilities and the bumper to bumper traffic distract from the ambience.

The drive up the mountain from the Port of Quepos to Manual Antonio is cluttered with people walking on the road or riding cycles of various configurations. The shops and bars along the way seem to have been slapped together with whatever building material happened to be available at the time. There is the usual jumble of overhead utility wiring supplemented by cables stretched high over the road to allow the local monkey population to get from one side of the road to the other as they go about their daily chores. It did not inspire confidence that our destination would match our expectations. Jose pulled the van to a stop in front of a low, sand-colored, one-story structure with an open arch leading into a very beautiful tropical mountain jungle garden. It is simply beautiful.

Falls Hotel is wonderful once you get past the entrance facade and step through the threshold into paradise. A hundred different shades of green greet the eye, as do red and yellow flowers in full bloom. Take a deep breath. The crisp mountain air is filled with a clean, fresh fragrance of the blooming gardenias and jasmine. The palm trees form a lush canopy home for songbirds, small monkeys, and lizards. Our expectations have been exceeded.

We head to the open-air bar, where we are greeted by the head waiter, Luis "Perro Grande." We become fast friends. We would have become friends faster, but we had four liters of Jack Daniels that we drank on our veranda, usually before dinner but not all at once. Dinner was simply wonderful.

The quay along the shoreline could have been lovely, but somehow it was not. It seemed a bit uncared for. What is billed as a new five-star hotel is under construction at the far end of the quay. It does not appear to be an active construction site. The pier where we are to meet the boat crew is heavily guarded, entrance is strictly controlled. There is a mix-up over our fishing license. J.R. deals with it; security is tight. The guards carry weapons.

We are allowed to proceed down the pier to meet our honcho, Justin. J.R. has his fly rod in hand. I have been assured there are other fly rods on board. The twenty-foot panga is anchored in the harbor. Justin says the crew is preparing the bait. Bait?

They take a while; at long last they get the bait the way they want and motor to the dock. All the other boats are long gone. There is about an hour to the blue water, twenty miles or so, a smooth ride out. The thought of bait is worrisome, but we think it might just be chum. Chum was used off Ocean City, Maryland, to attract a trophy White Marlin that hung over my fireplace afterward.

The Skipper of the Pez-Rey is of indeterminable age, in good shape, with dreadlocks colored blond, superb English, and cocky attitude. Says his name is Pepsi. Says he doesn't drink it. Alberto is the mate, older, darker, slim, a touch of gray, good English, and calm. Both came over from the Caribbean side, touted as great helmsman, fly fishers for tarpon, good with senior citizens, and neither has a toe ring. Why the hell do we care if they are good with senior citizens?

The boatmen have rigged the panga's two outriggers, port and starboard, with plastic teasers. Two spinning rods in their holders over the wheelhouse have more colorful teasers trailing behind the boat inside the outrigger's teasers, two spinning rods trailing eight- to ten-inch live Ballyhoo directly behind the boat with hooks. The panga is in troll speed, circling about twenty miles offshore in a peaceful deep blue ocean in search of sailfish on conventional spinning tackle. J.R. and I are in the front of the boat, scanning the horizon for whatever.

A reel sings in the back on the port side, J.R.'s side, and he hustles aft. Alberto hands him the spinning rod. A Mahi Mahi is on; reel, reel, and hold on, reel, reel, pump and reel, stay in the boat. A starboard reel comes alive, my side. We are doubled up. Pepsi gets me the rod, Mahi Mahi is running, stripping line, I'm holding on, leaning against the console, no shoes, no fighting seat, reeling as best I can bow to the fish and reel, pump and reel, again and again. The fish gets close, makes another run. J.R. lands his fish, flopped it at my feet. Mine is still running, over a hundred yards away, jumps, throws the hook, jumps free, and jumps again, free at last, free at last. All is good and fun. Dinner is in the boat.

No more than a few minutes later, another rod sings. Pepsi gets me the spinning rod, but I cannot get a grip on the left-handed spinning reel handle—one good sailfish gone.

Action slows for a short while, picks up again. J.R. lands a very nice sail, takes a good thirty minutes to boat him. He records the fight on the GoPro, we think. I miss another that Pepsi says is a big fish, well over a hundred yards away; tail walked forever, crank, crank, crank, left-handed, threw the hook. Curt Gowdy would have lost that fish, maybe. J.R. gets another thirty-minute workout and another big sailfish. We have six hookups, J.R. boats three.

Our first day chasing sailfish is a day we will both always treasure. J.R., by any measure, had one of his best days on the water, ever. All was good and fun, but it was not fishing with a fly.

The Falls restaurant is closed on Sunday, so we gave the Mahi Mahi to Johan to put in the freezer for dinner the next night. We enjoyed some Jack in the jungle then walked down the road to the nearest restaurant. It was a sports bar. We ordered pasta and watched the second half of the Super Bowl. Worst play call in the history of football. After eight hours on the water, I was tired, frustrated, and happy.

FEBRUARY 2015
THE REST OF THE TRIP

It turns out that Costa Rican fishing guides, like Irish fishing guides, maybe guides everywhere, share a lot in common: veracity, or lack thereof. If you are there, the fish you are after were there yesterday, and neither of these guys wore toe rings.

The morning after the Super Bowl was spent catching some bait fish, sardines or maybe anchovy, who cares. I got up before six o'clock for this. J.R. and I just sat there and watched. Finally, the bait buckets full, we could actually go fishing. I congratulated Pepsi for saving himself a trip to the grocery store.

This is our inshore fishing day, which is to say, we stay close to shore, fishing the inlets, bays, and just off the breakers. This is a much better day for me, and another great day for J.R. We caught magnificent roosterfish and yellowtail snapper for dinner, jacks, a ten pounder, and I don't remember what else. J.R. got two twenty-five to thirty-pound roosterfish, which were terrific fighters, much better than the sailfish except they do not jump, just pull and pull some more. Roosterfish are much prized for their beauty and fighting skills and need to be on any fly fishers' bucket list. They have been checked off ours, almost, except for the fly thing.

The end of another great day, Alberto is in a hurry to get home. I offer him a beer to slow down, and he declines; innards are rearranged. He says if I show up at the Double Hook Bar around seven o'clock, he will see to it that I meet some lovely young ladies of dubious moral fiber from most any country in Central America. I think I'll need to be there.

Dinner tonight is special. Perro Grande suggests Ceviche the Falls, made with the Mahi Mahi from Sunday prepared with a mixture of onion, chayote, carrot, red pepper, and cilantro. Sauvignon Blanc completes it.

Brandon prepares the freshly caught snapper for the main course tonight. We agree, even though J.R. has had cerviche every day, beginning at La Muni. Some Lynchburg whiskey is enjoyed on the veranda while Chef Brandon cooks up his magic on the fish, keeping the recipe to himself. We need some very deep breaths; some more Jack for medicinal purposes, a bottle of wine each with the fish and the Double Hook will have to wait.

February 5

We are not fishing; rather, we are horseback riding in the rainforest. We both had taken brief lessons on horseback riding before we got here. I don't know how long it had been since J.R. had been on a horse, but it must have been over forty years since I had climbed aboard one.

We need respite from the ocean. It is just the two of us with our guide Chi and his three dogs of indistinguishable origin, Mama Cass, Janis, and Elvis. Jimmy lives on the next farm over. A story unto himself, "China" tattoo on his left arm and no toe ring. He arrived in Costa Rica fifteen years ago from Argentina, where he had been a flight attendant on a small international airline. He was a world traveler, a man of the world, who now lives in one room in the stable. We just enjoy the jungle, no questions, and the ride down the stream on a once proud steed to a tall waterfall spilling into a wonderfully cold swimming pool.

The three dogs announced our whereabouts to any and all. Wildlife viewing was nil. We did encounter a long, skinny, green snake; Chi used the machete he was carrying to shoo it away. He said it was a Lady Snake. Photographs of the poisonous snakes of Costa Rica show precious little difference between an Eyelash Viper and a Lady Snake.

The view from the main house on top of the mountain is spectacular. The lady of the house served a delicious version of chicken and dumplings Costa Rica style. Bottom line is that we are now comfortable on horseback, and this opens a lot of other fishing opportunities. It is all beautiful and fun.

It is a rough road back to the Falls in time for our Mahi Mahi dinner, some Jack, and more wine. It is too nice and too comfortable to consider the Double Hook. I am tired. I think we must get up early again tomorrow.

By now it surely is Wednesday, but it's six in the morning, so who knows. We are going on a freshwater float trip on the El Savegre River. Justin picks us up at this ungodly early hour, and we drive forever, mostly over unpaved roads, into the wilds of mountains, through impoverished villages right out of a feed the children commercial. It is truly wonderful, beautiful, isolated, and awakening.

He delivers us to an African safari-type resort near the top of a mountain, eco-friendly and beautiful. Carlos, the South African owner, will be our guide on the float trip; nice and interesting guy. Costa Rica is home to one of the deadliest vipers in the world, the fer-de-lance, and one of the best health care systems in Central America. Several years ago, a doctor in San Jose recognized the symptoms. Carlos did not remember getting bitten. He barely survived.

The El Savegre provided a beautiful ride with several good whitewater rapids and some great bird watching. Fishing was almost awful;

caught two Machaca, did not need to put them on the reel, and a little snook. Over thirteen miles total. Machaca will not take a drifting fly. They will only strike the fly as it hits the water. A float trip of over a thousand casts, fly rods, finally.

It is up for debate whether the road to the resort or the white water or the horse ride or the very rough ride in the panga yesterday was the most physically demanding. They all required some whiskey when it was over. My vote is the panga ride, but the road is a close second.

Perro Grande and Brandon prepare the rest of our Mahi Mahi for dinner. If we allowed, we would be royalty. We meet some interesting folks on trips like this, and this one is no exception. A nice couple who are ranchers from Alberta, a girl-girl couple from Boston, a bunch of snobby Americans from north of the Mason-Dixon line, and a good guy from New Mexico who goes by Hoot and was also there to fish. J.R. explains the meaning of a rich widow to Johan and Luis and says that I need to meet one. Luis allows as how the owner of The Falls is just that. She is from Denver but happens to be here with her teenage daughter and does not imbibe in spirits. I never really found a proper opportunity to introduce myself. Don't get old. Hopefully, I'm just tired. The good news is I can sleep in, nothing till ten thirty tomorrow.

Our last day of fishing and only one more night at The Falls and Quepos. J.R. has launched a final plea to cast his fly rod to almost anything. He is reassured today is the day. This is not a good day, except we are in Quepos, Costa Rica. It is beautiful, and we are warm. We are happy. We have had a wonderful week. We are to fish inshore for half a day. Again, fishing for bait is necessary before we can really go fishing. The question is, why do we need bait to fish with a fly? So the frigate birds can steal it? Tijeretas cannot dive into the water. Their wings are not oiled as those of other seabirds are, so they steal food from other birds. They roost in trees and will hang themselves from the branches rather than starve to death.

Once we got started really fishing, I hooked on a big roosterfish; I was really into this one, determined, reeling left-handed is still unnatural, but determined. A few minutes into the fight, Pepsi turned hard to port and gunned the motor. Alberto is thrown face-first to the deck, almost overboard. I am damn near into the deep blue. The fish is gone.

Alberto allows as how my luck with the fish has continued. Later in the day, J.R. has a good fish on and again full throttle hard to port, just long enough so the fish escapes. I lost five hooked fish. J.R. lost a bunch, plus a very big roosterfish. This is really getting old. Another tooth-rattling ride to the dock would have ended our day, except we stopped to catch some more sardines or whatever. Pepsi needs to get himself a toe ring.

It is unbelievable to all our friends and fellow fisherman at The Falls that we were skunked. The snobby Americans from above the Mason-Dixon line smirked. The fact that anybody could say nada fish, no fish today, in this fishery is not possible. It defies nature, probably has never happened before, ever, full moon or no, in February or any other month, ever. We were not using fly rods.

Chef Brandon heard the hullaballoo over our misfortune from the kitchen and found us at the bar, licking our wounds. Amazingly, from somewhere, he produced a chart of Costa Rican fish, asked us if we could identify one that looked like a flounder. Did we eat it? Yes, we did. If he could get some would we like to eat it? Yes, we would.

Several drinks later, a bag full of fresh Costa Rican flounder was delivered to the kitchen. Brandon is a genius, a good guy, and a great fusion chef. Luis lives up to his nickname and makes a fabulous banana flambé for dessert; best flambé ever. Let the blue flame flow, flow, and flow. Perro Grande, Hoorah.

We are royalty. The good-byes are genuine.

The rest of my trip is pretty much downhill, almost. Someone stole my debit card info and had a good time in Ohio. I was unable to make phone calls or send or receive text messages. In the midst of all the banking confusion, my phone beeped with a text message, the first and only one in a week. Jackie, of Bay Point, saying my Jack Daniels Christmas lamp is on the bar at Club 19.

It is good to love and be loved, if only a little.

Spirit Airlines: never again. I was late leaving San Jose and missed my connecting flight. C.J. Smith was good with picking me up at midnight at BWI.

The west coast of Costa Rica is warm and wonderful, very little Caribbean influence. Perhaps, some year, after the Super Bowl and before the Daytona 500, we can do this again with fly rods.

¿Este es el viaje donde mis años alcanzaron conmigo? Debo averiguar si me he vuelto viejo. ¿Estoy cansado, pero viejo?

Pura Vida

SEPTEMBER 11, 2015
NEVER FORGET

The Orchard was in my rearview mirror by around midday. I'm headed to Lancaster on Virginia's Northern Neck, where my good friend Mike Wright bought a wonderful house overlooking the Corratoman River near the confluence of the Rappahannock River and the Chesapeake Bay. Having a house on the water with a dock already in place means a twenty-something-foot center console floating device, unobstructed fore and aft decks perfect for casting to stripers, becomes a necessity. The *Blue Duck* was nestled in its dock lift when I arrived in time for a brief evening cruise. No fish were found, but the steaks and cigars eased the disappointment.

A storm blew up and turned us around before we got to the Bay on Saturday morning. I headed out about noon and landed in Charlotte on my way to Greenville in time for an unremarkable dinner. Thought about getting up with Barbin but needed to be in Greenville early on Sunday.

Greenville is only ninety minutes from Fern Valley and some very big trout. The plan was to go fishing at the end of the insurance assignment on October 2, then head to Orangeburg on the fourth. That might have worked had it not started raining the week before the Clemson vs. Notre Dame game, and it did not stop. It was Biblical.

I might as well have been in Seattle or London. I figured the Sogue would not be fit to fish, so I canceled with Glad, and had I not headed to Orangeburg on Saturday, I would not have gotten there for a week. Didn't really matter as school was canceled, and I did not get paid for a week, but I was in Orangeburg. That was the good news; the bad news is I am in Orangeburg and cannot get out.

The South Carolina Midlands had floodwater ass deep to a fifteen-foot giraffe. Thirty miles of Interstate 95 were closed for over a week. Willie and Haggard's show in Florence was canceled. An opportunity missed.

Junior told me when I first arrived that Jay-bird was not working at the Chestnut until midweek. He's been drying out in the hospital for ten days. So, we went to The Bank Social Club. Nice-looking middle-aged blonde lady seated at the bar. I reintroduced myself to Ginger, and she remembered not the slow dancing, saying, "You're the one who twirled me." I did not go to the Chestnut Grill until Tuesday, and Jay-bird was working, his first day back. He was struggling. The branches of the trees along the stream bank had become black snakes. He recognized me as soon as I walked in and poured a proper welcome back, Jack on the rocks, without direction.

OCTOBER 31, 2015
A TASTE OF LUXURY

The earning part of this trip is almost over. I am tired. Seven weeks of 7:15 to 5:00 is difficult in and of itself. Throw in twelve to fifteen primary and kindergarten school teachers a day, many of whom have not had an adult conversation in years, plus an active social life, and I would have been tired thirty years ago.

Two nights before I was scheduled to leave, I met and began devoting several hours toward getting to know Holly, who was bartending at The Bank Social Club. Smoking is no longer permitted inside the bar. The first I learned there is a membership book was when a person of a more dubious character than the already dubious membership was denied service for not being a member, and that new membership was closed with a two-year waiting list. I suspect dues are collected upon having your name entered into the ledger. Holly said my name is in the book.

I admit to being a little droggie the next morning when Miss Savannah met me at a high school in the middle of a cotton field at 7:15. Waiting for and greeting us was a somewhat young, but not too young, teacher's aide, who wanted to enroll in disability insurance. She just discovered last week that she is pregnant—with a due date of next week. This and other close encounters nearly as ludicrous have taken a toll on my usual good humor, and I am glad this is my last day.

This will be my last night at the Chestnut Grill for dinner, with a fond farewell to Jay, and then I stopped by the HOP. Ms. Savannah was not there. Got a pizza to go, food is much better, and saved it. Then on to The Bank Social Club for one last shot at Holly. I told her I'd be back in a couple of weeks and asked if she would have dinner with me in Charleston. She said she would. There is very little I would enjoy more than being seen in Charleston with a very attractive lady half my age.

I am out of here. I probably could not have done this thirty years ago.

After dropping my computer off at my employer's office in Columbia a little after noon the next day, I had a difficult time staying awake on the drive to Charlotte.

My friend of forty years, Barbin, said he had to deal with his grandkids and could possibly get to the very fine Westin in Uptown South before seven. His call at 6:30 from the hotel bar found me asleep on the fourteenth floor. Several wines and delicious chicken sausage flatbreads later, we agreed to watch some football in one of his favorite haunts on Saturday afternoon. I was back to bed before nine.

Our longtime mutual friend, Cairns, whom I've been friends with since he was born when I was seven months old, could not come down off his mountain, so it was left for Barbin and me to check out the local talent. He is quite experienced and very knowledgeable about the local talent. We enjoyed some lunch and college football. NC State held its own for the first half against Clemson but wilted in the second.

I was on the road to The Orchard by seven the next morning. This time, I'm okay with heading home. Damn, I must be tired. Rain to the west was covering I-77 and I-81, so I opted I-85 to Greensboro, then Route 29 thru Virginia. It was a delightfully stress-free drive. I arrived in Frederick before the Red Horse opened, rapped on their door, and Stephanie opened and poured me a drink. I found Kat working at the TR and talked awhile; bought some breakfast food at Wegmans and was home by six.

NOVEMBER 21, 2015

"On the road again
        Goin' places I've never been
                Seein' things I may never see again,
And I can't wait to get on the road again." Willie Nelson, "On the Road Again," 1980.

Three weeks at The Orchard was a little more than I could handle. Did manage a dinner at the Wine Kitchen with the Widow McPherson. Prospects are bleak for restoring our relationship, something about commitment. Stocked up on fuel oil for the winter, did some other mundane stuff, and left to meet J.R. in Bryson City, North Carolina.

For some unknown reason, I hit the road later in the day than I should have and just made it to Roanoke before stopping for an uneventful evening. Why I surrender my highly developed and always reliable pathfinding ability to some irritating woman spuming misdirection from a box is beyond understanding. As a result, I saw more of the Smoky Mountains than I cared to and did not arrive until almost the cocktail hour. J.R. and I both agreed that we would disdain mundane chain accommodations in favor of some local flavor.

Through independent research, the Freymont Inn seemed to meet the criteria to make a good resting place for a couple of days before we head off to Georgia. It is truly a gem. A wonderful slice of Americana from a more genteel era, with comfortable leather chairs surrounding a large fieldstone fireplace, wood-burning and warm. A partially put together jigsaw puzzle lying on a large, heavy, wood community table in the great room garnered the interest of several guests, who were taking turns trying to make it whole.

There were many hikers of all ages challenging the six thousand feet of Clingmans Dome. The wife of a young couple from Florida allowed as how she saw the copperhead before her husband stepped on it but chose not to say anything, just let him go ahead. A lovely lady from Connecticut, whose mother, an aunt, and her husband showed up at an inappropriate moment. Another fisherman from Tennessee was with his family and not fishing but thought he might come back. Sometimes, a black bear would visit the patio.

The rather inexpensive room rate included two meals a day. Again, the meals were delicious, a most delightful surprise. The menu selections were varied, changed daily, and were totally generously delicious. The large bar off the dining room had all the usual accoutrement and attracted guests and locals alike. It was tended by a convivial local fellow of our generation. The pour was ample, and his stories were well told.

J.R. arrived earlier in the day to meet Mack Brown for some casting and fishing advice. Mack is highly regarded and widely known in fly fishing circles as a guide and fisherman. J.R. is working on getting his master's certificate in the art of casting a fly, and Mack's critique may be of some help in achieving that goal.

The next morning Mack arrived at the Freymont Inn early to gather us up, and J.R. introduced me to Mack.

We headed into Bryson City, where the Tuckasegee River was flowing high, brown, and fast. We found a slower and lower branch that runs through a city park, where the banks were open enough to allow for instruction in a new nymphing technique. The water was not fishable, but we all managed to land a few using the new technique, which is similar to using a Czech nymphing rig, but not exactly.

I am but a simple fly fisherman. Nymphing can be very productive but it is not my favorite form of fishing, so I really did not pay much attention to the intricacies of the Mack Brown system, and I don't know the Czech system from Adam. As best as I can figure, it involved a knotless attachment to the leader with a red or green "sighter" and a dropper fly. "Zatmakcent," spit.

"Mack reminds me of a southern version of the guide we had in Maine," I said after ordering dinner from the waitress that evening.

I had invited J.R. to join me for a week at Grants Camp near Rangeley, Maine, a couple of years after Jack and I had been there on a cast and blast trip. The Widow McPherson had backed out at the last minute, claiming her cats would miss her if she was gone that long. They are barn cats.

"You remember?" I asked.

"Yeah, he was good, put us on a lot of fish. I will never forget how he would tie the fly on the tippet by putting it in his mouth, twirling it around, and removing the fly tied on tight. Never heard of anybody doing that before, would not believe it if I hadn't seen it."

"The winters in western Maine are long," I said.

"Some of those landlocked salmon were citation fish; we should have submitted pictures," J.R. said.

"We will have to go back."

The waitress served our dinner.

The lovely lady from Connecticut and her entourage had checked out, and no new talent had checked in, but dinner was still excellent, and the stories at the bar were still good.

The next morning, the plan was for me to follow J.R. because his GPS was working better than mine, as we headed to Helen, Georgia. The plan fell apart at the end of the Fryemont Inn's driveway. I had to wait for traffic to clear and didn't see which road J.R. took at the overpass. I knew about where I was and about where Helen is, so I just followed my nose, and about lunchtime, I passed Harry's, so I knew where I was. There were no cars in the parking lot. I suspect ten dollars flat was not a successful business plan, particularly when the overseer of the plan tipped in at five hundred pounds.

We both got to Helen about the same time from different and opposite directions.

No condos this year. J.R. had rented a very nice house for the weekend in the same area as the condos through VRBO. Dinner was at the same German place as last year. The service was terrible due to a shortage of staff, but the food was again excellent.

The girls from last year were not at Paul's this year. The band was different and not as good, and there was a sparse crowd with few unattached ladies. The comely Amanda was no longer working there. We did not stay long.

On Sunday morning, we were on our way to Fern Valley on the Soque. As we were pulling into the Fern Valley driveway, J.R.'s phone rang. It was the rental agent wanting to know why our stuff was still in the house. We turned around. Turns out J.R. had only booked it for one night, which is why he thought it was such a good deal.

Glad was at church when we got back, and we were on the river, so we just waved hello. Fishing was not as good as last year, maybe because we tried the Mack Brown nymphing method, or our timing was just off. The fish were there. They were just not hungry or had become smart, as fish sometimes do.

As the sun was sinking behind the mountain and dusk descended on the river, I sent a text to Glad asking her to get a couple of bottles of wine out of J.R.'s truck and join me by the fire pit hard by the river. Oh, and to bring a corkscrew. She did. J.R. was wandering around somewhere downstream, still working on the nymphing technique.

Glad and I sat by the fire by the Soque and talked about life and old dogs as the golden trout began to rise to a hatch. Not much had changed. The wine was gone, and it was near dark. We had to head back to Helen, find a hotel for the night, and have some dinner at Mully's. There was some strange new rule about not eating at the bar. But Mully remembered us, and the rule was suspended for the evening.

We arrived in separate cars in Albany late Monday afternoon. The five-hour drive was uneventful except in Atlanta. No crazy thoughts of marriage either north or south of Atlanta, even while sitting in the ever-present traffic jam. I feel at home at the Pruitt's house. This year is no different. It is my job to not be underfoot. I took one day to drop down to Thomasville and replace a red wine glass that mysteriously disappeared from my collection.

Dinner is at Shannon's plantation house. Jake has slowed down some but looks good, doesn't care much anymore that the deer come right up to the house. An eight-point buck is keeping a close eye on his does. Franz and Mandy are there as usual, haven't changed any, still delightful. There is ample whiskey for the hardened palette. The wine is perfect, as is the turkey. J.R.'s health is not such a concern this year. Near emergency surgery to unblock his carotid arteries earlier in the year relieved some of the worries, but he had to miss the Willie Nelson concert in Tallahassee.

Thanksgiving Day, Julie offered the blessing; truly thankful.

JANUARY 30, 2016
STILL POINT POND, EASTERN SHORE, MARYLAND
GOOSE CAMP

The Winter of My Discontent, With Apologies to Shakespeare And Steinbeck.

"Mmm, old friends swapping lies of life and love…old friends looking up to see a bird…" Roger Miller & Willie Nelson. "Old Friends," 1982

Reminiscing over after-dinner libations last night, I think we all agreed that this is the fourth or fifth year we've rented the Barrett House on Still Point Pond, a little north and west of Chestertown on Maryland's beautiful Eastern Shore. There were two years at "Dickie's Place" south of here, prior to Still Point Pond. My memories of there are fuzzy. Perhaps more than a bit; seems I remember the first day of shooting pretty good, eighteen folded, nine confirmed from my Super Black Eagle, plus a mallard hen, for which I am remorseful. Don't remember kissing the coed waitress at the Blue Heron. I wonder if she is still there. Dickie came a cropper, much to our betterment.

I missed last year due to the flu or something akin to it. I need to be at Goose Camp.

This year, I arrived on Thursday about forty-five minutes into happy hour. Hill and Mike were there ahead of me by five minutes or so. Some years ago, after a very long courtship, Mike married Hill's very lovely daughter, Beverly, so they travel together quite often. Ron is in Saudi Arabia; not sure he needs the money. Mike's friend Bob rounds out the foursome for tomorrow. His first Goose Camp.

The welcome was like arriving at grandma's house for Thanksgiving, a warm welcome home again. I am as happy here as I was on the Upper Grand Lagoon at Bay Point. I am pretty sure I will not miss another year, if not here, someplace like it. I wonder if it's the view of the water or the taste of the wine. The water is frozen and covered with a dusting of freshly fallen snow. The wine celebrates life.

Goose hunting is ostensibly the purpose of this reunion. More like goose shooting. You just hide and wait, then all hell breaks loose. This year, Mike took over the role of retriever. The black Lab, Deke, had gotten too fat to fetch the fallen birds from the ice-covered pond. Mike is a big man, stands six feet three, and you could do an over-under wager on three hundred pounds. The pond is not very deep. But unlike Deke, Mike only has two legs to distribute the weight over. It took some real effort for him to crawl, soaking wet, on his belly back to dry land. Humbling, if not humiliating. Maybe it's really about something deeper than shooting.

I left my goose gun at home. Just being here is all I need, except I may become a bit too reflective, contented or discontented, in need of change. This is not a case of the grass is greener, more a case of attitude adjustment; perhaps this change of scenery will drive out the malaise. Winter storm Jonas dumped a ton of snow on the mid-Atlantic last weekend. Oil-burning furnace went out two days before Jonas. Repairman claims he rapped on the front door, apparently without much enthusiasm, as I never heard him. I slept in front of the kitchen fireplace. Snow was thigh high. I did not get plowed out for five days, just maybe cabin fever had an adverse effect on my attitude. I remember a time, not all that long ago, when the men of the town got together with their shovels and worked to open roads and driveways. They made sure folks had heat and groceries and that all was well with their neighbors. Precious little charity is left here; envy and ridicule abound. False humility is futile, be that as it is.

Always been that way.

Charlatans, shysters, and downright crooks trying to get in my pocket characterized January. December had been defined by everyone I encountered thinking I was old and therefore stupid, including the money-grubbing orthopedic doctor and his lame attempt to replace my knee. I fired him in his own office.

Well, maybe not everyone. A chance meeting with Miss O'Malley may result in another picnic. Holly said she'd have dinner with me in South Carolina. And then there's Kat.

Kat still loves me and I her. Christmas on Friends Creek was again special. She brought her violin. Lobster bisque, fine wine and selections of Handel's Water Music as the creek flows in the background. We threw a line into unfishable waters just so we could say we did. She is re-dedicating herself to her violin.

Cabin fever was reaching the critical stage. Not yet terminal, but it is The Orchard. Still Point Pond is healing. Saturday morning sunrise is blinding off the frozen pond. Sky is high and blue, so shooting will not be so good. By lunch yesterday, snow squalls and low hanging clouds shooters had their limit. The larder will be full again this year.

Still Point Pond is awash in sunshine. I am warm, and it is happy hour. Mike, Hill, and Bob left the house at seven in the morning; it was cold and dark. The shooters returned at seven in the evening; it was cold and dark. Six geese for the freezer. Bless the poor souls.

Appetizers of goose breast bits wrapped in bacon will not continue the downward trend of my weight necessitated by overindulgence.

Dinner was served rather late, I think, about four or five hours into happy hour. The wine pour was a tad heavy. Hill and Mike continued refreshing my memory of forgotten Goose Camps; age, and the wages of sin. I guess we ran out of wine. May have killed my last goose, will leave that open for further consideration.

Sunday morning found a haze behind my eyes. I suspect more than just mine. The smell of red pepper hot on the stove cleared the haze. Mike has prepared goose sausage patties and some wonderful egg dish as a farewell breakfast. The stories continue of goose camps before it became

Goose Camp. Plans were made for Trout Camp on Friends Creek in April. I opted not to finish the Goldschlager story; decorum rules, not a morning story. It will wait until after the first drink next year. This is, after all, Goose Camp.

I will be heading back to The Orchard. As usual, I don't want to go. In a couple of weeks, I will head south again. The new neighbor who is fixing up the house just across the street noticed my car parked by the barn. I had given him a glass of water on a hot day last summer. He stopped over to welcome me back, felt it was cold in the kitchen, and fixed my furnace in fifteen minutes.

Flying out of Charlotte to Cancun on the nineteenth, where I will meet up with J.R. and head further south to Pesca Maya, silver ghost on the fly, for a week. A couple of days in Orangeburg before take-off and after could be a lot of fun, taking Holly to Charleston for dinner or whatever. Fern Valley is not that far away.

It is good to love and be loved, if only a little.

FEBRUARY 19, 2016
ASCENSION BAY, MEXICO

"And now as I wander, my thoughts ever stray. South of the border, down Mexico way." Gene Autry, "South of the Border," 1939

I decide to fly directly to Cancun from Charlotte. It worked out great, but not exactly as planned.

J.R. had arrived in Cancun earlier in the day and was at the lobby bar of the Marriott Casa Magna when I arrived via prearranged transport. Flawless. Dinner is at the La Capilla Argentine in the hotel. Steaks of a different cut were superb. The couple dancing the tango made it like being on the set with Hope and Crosby in *The Road to Rio*. The girl dancer had bad, cheap-cigarette breath.

The morning sun arrived early, bright in a cloudless sky. The wind was blowing on the beach, and a Bloody Mary or two at the pool bar prepared us for the perfectly uninteresting trip to Tulum. I am not sure what

I was expecting, but it was disappointing and uninteresting. Familiar chain stores jammed into spaces more suited to small family businesses than big-box warehouse stores.

The tropical sun warms stiff joints, and old bones don't hurt. I am not tired. Macabi on the fly; J.R. Pruitt and I have embarked on another adventure. As best as I can figure from chronicles and memory, this will be our thirtieth or so. Most involve casting a fly, but not all. The first was on the East Branch of the Delaware in April 2002. This one will be special. I tell him so.

The original plan, thought up last year in Costa Rica, was to go after redfish in Louisiana between the Super Bowl and the Daytona 500; must avoid becoming one-dimensional. The plan changed in November while chasing trout in the Great Smoky Mountains of North Carolina.

J.R., or more likely, his wife Julie, suggested that we could go to Louisiana anytime, but we are getting a little late in life to pass up a bone fishing trip to Pesac Maya Lodge in Mexico. They are running a deal through Yellow Dog Fly Fishing and given our respective ages and J.R.'s general health, we should really make a trip out of it while we are still able. J.R. has fished the flats of Belize several times, as well as the Boca Paila flats once before from a different lodge. My flats experience was only a half-day out of the Cheeca Lodge. I was traveling alone and was fortunate to have dinner in the bar before it burned down destroying the priceless memorabilia of Ted Williams, George H.W. Bush and Curt Goudy. I loved it. Sight fishing flats is like hunting with a fly rod. Hemmingway's Pilar was in a museum just down the road.

FEBRUARY 20, 2016

The ancient Mayans (200–900 AD) were renowned for building roads connecting cities hundreds of miles apart without curves, spear-straight lines through the jungles. It is plumb straight from Cancun to Tulum for about ninety minutes, where we hang a left onto another straight road with speed bumps every ten yards, which is littered with European tourists on bicycles emerging from miles of back to back cabana hotels. The pavement runs out about when the hotels do, and for no apparent reason, we stop by a small opening in the jungle. It opens to a path; a Purple Gallinule hustles across the trail ahead of us as we head toward a dock where a flats boat is tied up. Someone we don't know tells us that is not our boat. Our stuff has found its way to the dock. Our driver is not to be found. We settle in a small clearing in the jungle and wait. Every now and again folks emerge through the trees and disappear toward the dock. They seem to have no real purpose, but there is a rhythm to their comings and goings. Eco-Green tourists disembark from guide boats all smiles. A group of fishermen returning from Pesac Maya offer full-throated lies about their Grand Slams, wish us good luck. Our stuff is still on the dock.

Our driver appears from parts unknown, loads our stuff and us onto the newly arrived flats boat for the hour ride to a dock that leads to a path through the jungle for a good half mile. The trees are full of orioles. Guides with wheelbarrows cart our gear to the lodge. We are directed to our room, Seclusion, bang on a bluff above the Gulf's pounding surf.

The Pesca Maya Lodge is located midway down what amounts to the outer banks off the east coast of Quantana Roo, south of Yucatan. The main lodge is where meals are taken, and the bar is open twenty-four hours a day. The beer truck is sometimes a day late. There are two small camp dogs; one is quiet. The entire compound is powered by wind and solar with diesel backup and is just a tad fishing-camp rustic.

The communal dining table fostered the opportunity for interaction with our fellow lodge mates, who were more than a little interesting. Shrimp and rice and a nice white wine fostered the convivial conversation.

Four others, all from Denmark, accompanied a beautiful blonde, Hannah, her husband, Kip, and their friend, Kite, a distinguished gentleman of my vintage who was a highly accomplished storyteller. They come every year and are leaving the next day but made wonderful companions for the evening. They were replaced by five guys and a girl from Cleveland. Ravishing Ruby, a forty-something, is an attractive blonde, who also comes every year with her friend. She has had trouble adapting to casting in the wind. J.R. is a certified casting instructor, and I bragged heavily on his skills and offered his services to provide some advice. She was pretty but reminded me of the voice on my Range Rover's GPS, which if I'd had a gun, I would have shot it somewhere in Montana. Adrian and his son Will are keen fishermen from London who are quite fond of fishing in Russia.

At some point, and I don't remember why, we had to declare straight or not. We set that straight, straight away. I suspect Ravishing Ruby. There were day-trippers from Denver and some from the Netherlands, some stray old hippies and some I did not meet. Most are repeat visitors to Pesca Maya, and all were very fascinating conversationalists. We held our own.

FEBRUARY 21, 2016

Breakfast is at 0700, huevos y carne and a fruit juice of some variety.

Senor Martin, the head honcho, is an ebullient fellow and runs a very efficient operation. He introduces us to Daurin, our guide for the week. All with Mayan blood, no matter from how long ago, are about a half an Englishman tall with straight coal-black hair. Daurin is almost as wide as he is tall; good English, a brick of a man with a square face charred by the sun except for the light brown raccoon mask behind sunglasses, it's hard to age him. By 0800 we are on a flats boat with Venancio, the first mate. He claims to be 41, with six children. He has a lightly tanned angular face and looks to be not a day over eighteen, a fact he attributes to never smoking or drinking beer. He is slight of build, wire cables for muscles, and has six words of English; neither wore toe rings.

We headed north to the Boca Paila Lagoon into a steady twenty-knot wind whipping up two-foot swells. A Grand Prix course cuts through the mangroves. Daurin, who thinks he is Juan Pablo Montoya, got a little loose on a hard left; slowed down. He dropped anchor in a somewhat calm cove. I hooked my first bonefish. I told J.R. this was not exactly what I had expected. The reel did not sing and landing it seemed too easy. The next hookup was more like what I had been told would happen. The reel sang all the way to the backing in about ten seconds. Now

I am happy. The wind is death to casting a fly. Daurin keeps us casting with the wind, and it is still difficult. "Muscle it," he scolds. The casting platform has no rail, nothing to brace you against the wind, so it's awfully easy to cast yourself off the boat. Large, high roll casts seem to work best; I caught bonefish after bonefish, saved the fly, and stayed dry.

FEBRUARY SOMETHING, 2016

The trip continues, one day becomes the next. Flats are called flats for a reason, enormous seascapes with the unvarying character of flat water; a fringe of mangroves here and there add texture. One mangrove looks like every other mangrove. Still, there is a sense of mystery, excitement over what they hold in their shallow waters. There is nothing else, just blue sky and dark green water swarming with life. We saw stingrays as big around as a fifty-gallon barrel.

Daurin got us a new boat that had a rail on the casting deck but was devoid of any modern navigation devices, not even a compass. The mangroves were not all the same to him. The wind was still blowing hard. We headed south across a rough Ascension Bay; boat had covered foam seats.

"You know, J.R., these fiberglass things sometimes break in half."

"Thought you wanted to die quick."

"Yeah, but not until I catch an Atlantic salmon."

"You won't do that here."

Maybe next year, I thought.

Almost to Belize, into coves somewhat protected by mangroves. Still, the wind was a challenge. I had to hold the rail and reel; nearly got blown off the deck.

Daurin was on the pole directing blind casting: ten o'clock to you, muscle a short back cast, sidearm, forty feet. Venancio coached by my side on the foredeck: strip, strip, quick; strip, strip, quick; hard strip, tip up, fish on. A well-seasoned toothpick held tightly between my teeth, seven were hooked, netted, and released before lunch. I stayed dry.

We took turns in the morning. I did not fish after lunch. Pruitt was not having a good day, nothing in the morning. He has fished the flats for many years, several trips to Belize and to his favorite, Long Island, the Bahamas with Docky Smith. Today, everything was wrong; the wind, the fly, the leader, the cast. He may have offended the ancient Mayan gods. The curse has returned.

"You did it yesterday," Daurin encouraged him, but nothing helped.

A delicious cut of sea bass and another nice white wine, and things got better.

Ravishing Ruby ditched her normal Patagonia fishing outfit when arriving for dinner or maybe a casting lesson, thinking she was instead at a Cancun casino. Coiffed hair, painted lips, long lashes, stiletto sandals, and a ruffled sleeveless white blouse cut to the waist, where it met black leotards with large oval cutouts exposing lily white skin above and below both knees, inside and out.

The elder of the Englishmen won the game of musical chairs to sit next to her. Her friend took dinner at the far end of the table. J.R. could not catch a cold.

The wind would remain an issue all week. Daurin put the boat in positions that allowed for good, strong side-armed casting and great catching every day. One afternoon, the wind relegated us to trolling for barracuda. J.R. caught the first one on a rod he had built himself at Seele, a rod builder in Pennsylvania. An 8-foot, 8 inch 10-weight, spun the glass himself and everything. It's his first fish on that rod. Apologies to Santiago, only his head remained when he got to the boat. A few moments later, my first one suffered the same fate. We managed to boat eight in their entirety, dinner for the guides and the best ceviche appetizer ever.

A storm blew in from the west late in the afternoon, bringing the sweet smell of the tropics on its breeze. It quickly passed. We watch the rising of the evening star, so large, with a full moon hanging by her side on the eastern horizon. It was the purest and mildest of a starlit February night.

The Mayan guides have made their ancient forefathers proud. Boating forty bonefish on the fly in a few hours, plus a whole bunch of jacks, lookdowners, and a permit is damn exceptional, that was our last day. J.R. says landing bonefish, jack, and a permit in the same day is a

Slam of some sort.

The best we could figure, the week brought eight different species to the net, all on the fly. We hunted snook to the north and tarpon to the south, but none were to be found. The guides said they were here yesterday. Today, the water was too dark. Not too dark for a lone dolphin to find our boat, though. Daurin cut the motor, and the dolphin stopped to play, circling and snorting for a quarter of an hour before continuing its solo journey.

While removing the fly from one of J.R.'s bonefish, a barracuda exploded out of the water from under the boat, taking the fish, line, and fly, missing only Daurin's hand. He took a seat and had a smoke. We only needed two more bonefish to make forty for that day, and J.R. landed them without incident. Vinny and I had become a team. A nice size jack had gotten into my backing, and I lost count of my share of the forty, pretty much wore me out. The one and only permit of the week brought forth a well-articulated "you lucky son-of-a-bitch" from someone who had been trying all his life to catch one. A permit is highly coveted by fly fisherman. Venancio offered a proud smile and handshake. I happily accepted.

XI-A AIN SAMCI
FEBRUARY 26, 2016

Breakfast Is at 0700, Huevos y Carne

This was our last breakfast with our new friends from Chagrin River Outfitters.

Yesterday was a seminal day. J.R. and I have fished together many times in many places. There is this annoyance that has followed us. It found us here a couple of days ago. It may not have begun on our first trip to Alaska, but it was there that it manifested itself. When one of us is having a good day, the other is not. There he was fishing from one side of the guide boat. I was fishing the exact same rig from the other side. We were back to back. He was pulling in salmon on every cast. I was not even getting a nibble.

"Bart, what are you doing wrong?" Whitey the guide asked.

J.R. chimed in, "He's holding his jaw wrong."

I found a well-seasoned toothpick in my jacket pocket, stuck it between my teeth, and began hauling in salmon one after the other. I fished that whole week with the same toothpick.

Earlier in the week, I had a great morning, and J.R. had a bad afternoon. Yesterday, J.R. had gotten off to a good start early. I began slowly, found another well-seasoned toothpick, and caught up with him. We pretty much ended the day even. The curse was exorcised, again.

We had been fishing near the Chagrin guys for most of the week and were within earshot yesterday. They said, "You guys must have caught fifty fish." Exactly right, my friends. Bigger fish of each variety may or may not have been caught by others, but no one caught more of each.

LOS DIOSES MAYAS SONIRO SOBRE NOSOTRAS

I know precious little of the ancient Mayan culture. Daurin and Vinny, along with all the other guides out of Pesca Mia, made it perfectly clear they are of Mayan descent. I felt a little apprehensive about penetrating the mysteries of the sacrificial ruins found in the mangroves. It's humbling and inspirational to be in the presence of a monument to the religious superstitions of extinct civilizations.

We had more Jack Daniels than we could drink, left half a liter on the house bar.

We reversed the journey of last week. Daurin must have been happy with his tip as he volunteered to be our flats boat driver back to Tulum. An uneventful trip lands us at the Cancun airport in about three hours. Bid a fond farewell to J.R., found my way to the wrong departure gate, fell asleep, and damn near missed my business class flight back to Charlotte.

My car was parked at the Marriott Courtyard. They were very quick to pick me up at the airport. I ran into my old friend Bolivar on the way to the pick-up zone. He said if I start up my old company, he is available. Marriott's driver delivers me directly to a much cleaner car than I had left.

I put my foot to the floor and made it to the Chestnut Grill in time for a late-night dessert and drinks with a cleaned up, straightened out Junior Jay-bird was working and looking good. Peggy Sue came over to say she is no longer engaged to Junior Hmmm. Holly said she was not well and would get with me tomorrow. We closed the place.

Late in the morning, I stopped by Junior's spirits shop but did not buy anything; instead, I gathered him up and headed to the golf course. The last time I played golf was late in October of 2014, and it was nine holes with Junior. Borrowed clubs, no practice balls, one practice swing and two hours later, counted fifty strokes on the same ball, which became a flat rock and skipped over the pond on the sixth. But I'm not unhappy as I went bogey, par, bogey on the last three holes. Junior played the ninth from places it has never been played from before, lost count of his strokes sometime after he found his ball down by the stop sign. If there had been a wager, he would still have won, maybe.

Junior had a date in Charleston; Holly says she is up and about and will meet me at five o'clock. Some long time after five, she says to give her a minute she was on her way. Ordered dinner for one and had another long talk with Jay-bird. She has the veracity of an Irish fishing guide, probably wears a toe ring. Ms. Savannah was not at the HOP, stopped by

The Bank Social Club and had a beer with Thomas Braxton Bryant IV. He is to go quail hunting tomorrow; wild birds on a Sunday. I love the South.

There is no other place to go. I am going to The Orchard.

FEBRUARY 28, 2016
ON THE ROAD TO THE ORCHARD

Kat has had a terrible week. Lost a dear friend in a one truck accident and broke down while playing the music at his memorial service. I made great time to Frederick. Found her working at TR, listened a long time, and told her I loved her.

I arrived at The Orchard last night. Maybe could have lived here happily this time around with a good woman and a bird dog. It became only the dog, and he too is now gone. Yet still, this place calls to me. Wandering the fields and woods as a child is a legacy that endures and inspires my spirit to this day.

The seasons did not matter so long as the fields were free of snow. One time they were not, it was maybe a foot deep, and the girl down the street, some other kid, and I thought it would be a good idea to walk cross-country to Westminster, seven miles away. It was a shortcut for ten-year-olds. At her funeral two years ago, the old people reminded me of the time Doris, some other kid, and I got lost in the snow back of town. We were not lost; we knew where we were. It was not where we wanted to be. When I heard she was in the hospital, I sent her a card reminding her people from The Orchard do not die. Her husband said it made her laugh. She died anyway. She had moved away.

It is true the same people would still be at the general store today if it was still open, but it is not. The storekeeper is still there, it's just not open anymore.

Beginning at the end of World War II, suicides became the primary cause of death, preceded by boredom. Tired of living, Mr. Kudlow grew tired of not looking before crossing the street on his way to the general store and shot himself. Most chose to hang, a half dozen or more.

Walter Newton's father had a farm on which he had an old black electric car, shaped like a stove-pipe top hat, and grew apples. I am pretty sure he opted to hang. Walter himself chose the same. All were men; women went to church, choice of three in town. Most women were not into killing themselves. Men who had seen war were more apt to.

Maybe could have lived here happily…

OCTOBER 1983
STATTSBURG, NEW YORK
LAST NINE FREE

The Khobar Towers bombing was still fresh in the news. I had been at Pondview Kennels a day or two. I don't remember exactly how long or exactly why I was there. I didn't have a dog in training and had not for close to ten years. Pondview had become a sanctuary for me. A place to unpack stress. I would come here several times a year, whether I had a dog here or not. Pondview was one of those places where everything was honest. There was no pomposity, over-blown egos didn't stay long. Even when I was not the best shot, Jerry tolerated my gunning. The only requirement was to love flushing dogs. Well, the honest part is almost true.

Pondview Kennels is an eighty-acre dog training utilitarian paradise in upstate New York. Staatsburg is not near anywhere and Pondview sits on the only unpaved road in Dutchess County. There are no neighbors, but the track at Saratoga was an easy drive. Back then it was sparse, and if you were anybody who was somebody in the flushing dog world, you would have been there.

Mornings were special, you could wake up to find anybody from the flushing dog world asleep on the couch, in the La-Z-boy, or on the floor. This morning I awoke in the guest bedroom. There was no one asleep in the living room. Jerry was making coffee, fried eggs, and bacon in a cast iron skillet. Jerry had been sober now for the better part of a decade, and to keep his mind straight had graduated from Le Cordon Bleu Culinary Arts School. He specialized in Italian cuisine and American hospitality. Having cocktails with the CEO of U.S. Steel, his wife, and their black Lab courtesy of the Queen was run of the mill stuff. Talbot Radcliffe came for the food and the dogs. Talbot invited me to a shoot on his North Wales estate, home of the famous Saighton line of springers. There are five of his Saighton's in the Bird Dog Hall of Fame. He wanted a king's ransom. I ended up with two of his books, one autographed. The only time I fished the pond was with Teddy Ross, enough said. A couple of times I didn't get there in time for the spare bedroom, ended up on the couch. Budweiser was in the basement.

Puppy training was the priority for this morning. I was the only gun in the place. There was no need for an expert gunner. All I needed to do was hit the sky. I could do that. The afternoon rolled around, and we brought out a couple of the older dogs for some gun work. The drill was that each dog got two birds. The gunner was supposed to kill each bird providing an opportunity for the dog to retrieve and bring the dead bird to hand. Gun dog training is a process, it takes time. "Nine women cannot make a baby in one month." I was still the only gun in the place. Two dogs and four pigeons later, all were brought to hand. We decided to call it a day.

We headed back to the truck parked by the upper field where we were surprised to find a paying client wanting to run their dog. They were a father-daughter duo, dressed out of the Abercrombie & Fitch Madison Avenue store, Connecticut okay and Darien rich. They should have spent a little less money on their clothes and a bit more on their dog. He was a good looker. He may or may not have been a springer. They were too well dressed to be springer people. Jerry planted the first bird. The good-looking dog may or may not have flushed it, but it flushed. I shot it at about twenty yards. Some long time later Jerry picked it up and put it in his game bag. The second bird was dizzied and planted close at hand. The good-looking dog ran over it and it flushed, scaring the good-looking dog half to death. I did not shoot. Broke the side by side, hung it over my shoulder and headed back to the truck.

"What the hell you doin'?" with both arms raised above his head. He could have been heard a mile away. Jerry was not pleased.

"Sorry Jerry, I have been in the Middle East the last two weeks killing assholes and I'm tired of killing."

Jerry dropped his arms, shrugged his shoulders, looked at his paying client, and whispered, "He works for the CIA." An identity given to me back when Smoke was in training here, and before Jerry took up cooking, to impress the lovely young ladies in the bars of Hyde Park.

The Connecticut OK clients gathered up their dog, declined an invitation for a sociable beer back at the house, and went home.

I'm guessing it was Davetta Curtis, she bred Smoke, who told me Jerry was the best trainer around and he might consider working with Smoke because he owned Jonell, Smoke's sire. Must have been sometime in 1985. I don't remember how I found out about field trials or even where to find one, but I did. I showed up at my first field trial in a three-piece Brooks Brothers pinstripe, Burberry trench coat, and wingtips; was ignored till I got Smoke out of the car and got in line behind a bunch of other dogs. This caught the attention of some official-looking person who questioned, who are you and what the hell are you doing? I explained that I was looking for the guy who owned Jonell, think he goes by Jerry. I was rather rudely instructed to put myself and the dog back in the car and wait until the trial was over to find Jerry. I did, and Jerry found me in due course. I told him Smoke was the son of Jonell and I was moving to Maryland. I wanted to hunt with him and would he please take him for a month or so and train him to hunt. Jerry allowed as how he would consider it and I should bring Smoke to Pondview to check the place out and so he could evaluate Smoke.

I did all that, but when Smoke and I got to Pondview Jerry was not to be found and nobody knew when he would be back. Whoever was there suggested I take Smoke to Jerry's brother's place until Jerry could be found. I did, and Bobby took Smoke in, didn't want to and said so. I begged, he promised to deliver him to Jerry as soon as possible.

At the time Jerry shared the one story, two-bedroom rancher with Cookie, who was a wife or girlfriend and partner in training. Smoke was six years old and had never hunted a bird of any kind. Jerry was occupied with Pondview's Left at the Light on his way to his first of two National Field Trial Championships.

He was not bashful about expressing his opinion regarding judges, handlers, gunners, breeders, other people's dogs, the Parent Club, and training six-year-old dogs with no experience. But he took Smoke in. Didn't want to, and said so, didn't go looking for him when he climbed over the eight-foot chain link fence in his kennel. Smoke came back the next day and things got better between them. Jerry put a roof on his run. Two individuals, who were both passionate, both stubborn, both opinionated, both demanding excellence from the other, made their peace.

With Smoke safely stashed at Pondview, what would become my most recent ex-wife and I moved from New Jersey to a rented farmhouse in the middle of a three-hundred-acre farm in Maryland. Fifteen years of paying tolls had lost its charm. It was just about far enough from my hometown to discourage visitors, and the lane was a half mile of dirt.

Jerry and Smoke bonded. There was the lower field and the upper field cultivated for field trial training. Jerry kept a pigeon coup near the car park by the upper field. It was big enough to stand up straight and catch the pigeons with a fish net at the end of a long pole. It had one door and no windows. It was hardened against coons, foxes, snakes, and coyotes. It was not Smoke proof. Somehow Smoke pried the door open as Jerry and I were standing there enjoying a beverage. Jerry evicted him by the nape of his neck, no birds escaped, except the one Smoke had in his mouth.

He ran Smoke in a Cocker Club Trial and got him a ribbon, got Bernie Castellani to breed him. Jerry said he'd gone as far as he could go with Smoke, so I brought him home to the farm. He road shot gun with his head on my lap the whole way home. There would be no more field trials. We had the pick of the litter, and Jerry chose a liver and white dog, with dark brown eyes. Smoke welcomed his son without hesitation. Remington of Pondview joined our trek as soon as he gained some confidence that we would come back.

Remy went back to Pondview for serious field trial training when he was ten months old. Our hopes were high. He had grown tall with a sturdy chest, a broad back, and a good noise. He had shown a lot of promise walking the fields with Smoke and me, and the genes were very good. Jerry was still concentrating on Lefty, so he gave Remy to Cookie for training. She was good, and she and Remy bonded. Cookie won a ribbon with him at the Bushy Hills Puppy Stakes. Hopes got higher. Cookie got shot and left. Remington refused to retrieve for Jerry. Don Candy was the gun and witnessed this absolute refusal. I asked Don, "what do I do now?" He said, "take him home. "Training ended. There would be no more field trials.

I brought Remy home to the farm and his first chance to retrieve was a half-shot pheasant, flew five hundred yards deep into the woods. Remy gave chase. It took him a quarter hour to bring it to hand.

THE EARLY YEARS

There was not much overnight travel in the early years on the farm; that would come later. After breakfast I would take my morning coffee with Smoke on a two-mile jaunt over the hills. We had an irregular route. He was close to being seven and still full of himself. For the first time in his life he could run free — unfettered. Except for the time he escaped from his run at Pondview Kennels.

A boy needs a dog, or at least I thought so. We were living in Connecticut and the most recent ex-wife found a litter near Hartford with only one left. She brought him home with a fist full of AFC and FC pedigrees from Jonell and to more Saighton's and J-J's and Shrewsbury's and Denalisunflo's then I have seen since. We had ourselves an honest-to-God, more than we could handle bird dog. I named him Blue Ridge Smoke.

Our house did not have a yard. A boy and his dog need a yard. We found another house that had a bigger yard, still no fence, so we strung high wire and a lead, and he escaped from that, once got his ass run over by a car and other time got the lead hung up on a rock wall deep in the woods while flushing ducks off a pond, and barked forever till I got home and tracked him down.

Employment necessitated a move to New Jersey; found a house with a swimming pool and a fence. He loved the pool, took to the diving board like an Olympian, dug under the fence, erected a better fence — jumped it. His passion for freedom was matched by a fiercely aggressive protective nature. It was never a good idea for a non-family member to raise their voice or make a sudden move toward a family member. He gave no warning, no bark, no growl, just attack. No one ever got hurt, scared yes, but not bit. It was always quick and short, enough to change the behavior of the perpetrator. When the boy was about fifteen; got stone cold drunk at one of his friend's house, vodka. The friend's father delivered him to our basement door, laid his unconscious body on a mattress on the basement floor. Smoke laid down next to him and stayed there till the middle of the next day.

One night we came home to the New Jersey house to find the lock on the kitchen door had been violated but not disabled. The door's window glass was broken. The shards were on the ground outside the kitchen. Smoke had a bloody nose. Before we moved to the farm, Smoke and I spent our Saturday afternoons sharing the couch and my beer while watching college basketball on TV. Budweiser was his favorite. He soon tired of Dickie V.

THE FARM

On a very pleasant summer morning, what was then still my family and a friend were taking the dogs for a long walk across the hay fields. Smoke was about a hundred yards off when Remy got into a tussle with a groundhog and was losing the battle. The varmint had latched onto his throat and was not about to let loose. Yelps and yells and screams of profanity got Smoke's attention, and much like the cavalry, he came charging in at full speed, grabbed the varmint by the head, and crushed — then tossed it aside. Without so much of a howdy-do, he returned to what he had been doing before becoming John Wayne. Remy was bleeding badly. I carried him out of the field and drove him to the vet for stitches and shots.

Fredneck Sam lived a couple of farms over and liked to bird hunt. Sometimes we would hunt his farm and sometimes mine. We had hunted together two or three times. There was something about him that I didn't much trust. One day as were gearing up at my place Sam asked, "How much are those dogs worth?" Remy and Smoke were still running around loose in the short grass waiting for us to head on down the hill. I slipped two high brass #6 shot shells into the side-by-side. "Sam…" looking him straight in the eye, "they are worth your life," and snapped the gun closed with vigor. "Let's head on out." Smoke didn't much trust Sam either. Before the day was over, he had Sam "treed" on top of a round bale of hay. I don't know what Sam did to deserve this, but Smoke was not about to let him off the hay bale. I got a lead on Smoke and took him to the house. That was the last time Sam came around.

Deep into November 1988, a day of high blue sky, air warmed by the sun to the high-fifties, a light breeze off the mountains, I was halfway to Baltimore on I-70. The not yet most recent ex-wife was not home, both dogs were, no idea where the boy was. I think in Oxford, diddling everything but his books. I realized the absurdity of having a business meeting under these conditions. Turned around, went back to the farm, called in sick, changed into jeans and boots, wiped down the side-by-side, grabbed a handful of shells, and called the dogs to a semblance of order. They knew as soon as I grabbed the gun this was not just another walk; could not get them out of the house fast enough.

They raced through the mowed grass down the hill toward the pond, whistled them to "hup." "Sit" sounds too much like shit, a word heard frequently in training. We hunted a small covert, nothing, then into another mess of multiflora roses, honeysuckle, and thorn trees, again nothing. Gathered them up, crossed the crest of the hill, turned them loose. Remy worked the tall grass, Smoke jumped into a honeysuckle cover. Out came a full-grown rooster, helicoptered straight up, climbed high and fast going away left to right, thirty yards in the blink of an eye.

The last half of his life, Blue Ridge Smoke ran free on the farm, never straying too far, except once. A late afternoon thunderstorm blew in while the dogs were out in the yard. A particularly close clap of thunder got my attention, and when I went to bring them in, Smoke was gone. Sometimes an old dog will do that. I walked all three hundred acres in the pouring rain, whistling and calling his name. I looked in every multiflora rose, in every patch of switchgrass, and every bed of honeysuckle vine. Nothing. I expanded the search, miles of the local roads, expecting to see him lying by the side of the road. I gave up near dark. One last look over the hill, and there, a quarter of a mile off, I saw a struggling hunk of liver and white trying to climb out of the stream over the bank. I gathered him up, carried him home, cleaned him up, and held him as he fell asleep.

After a time, Smoke stopped the morning walk at the top of the hill where the mowed grass ended, sat down, and watched as Remington and I made the circuit. He had grown gray, and his eyes were cloudy and sad. What may have been the last wild pheasant in Frederick County is mounted with a plaque saying, "Flushed and Retrieved by Smoke, November 1988." Remington honored the flush.

The plan was to stay on the farm for a year. The dogs and I loved it. Some seven years later a move became necessary. We bought a home with a small, fenced-in, formal garden in Frederick's Historic District. Business required extensive travel; long periods being gone. Smoke was too tired to escape. He just kind of gave up.

Remington got fat, caught something he would not have caught on the farm, died in a vet's kennel while I was traveling and could not get home in time to say goodbye. I have his ashes. Maybe I'll take them back to the farm before I die.

According to at least one member of the Bird Dog Hall of Fame, Blue Ridge Smoke was the best dog I'll ever have. In his fourteen years with me, I learned more about life, love, duty, responsibility, freedom, and honesty than I ever learned from anyone, anywhere, anytime. He asked no quarter and gave none; he did not suffer fools — gladly. He did not chase his tail, and if you could not do your job, as good as he could do his, respect was not unconditional. Affection was not his strong suit.

Comparisons are inevitable. Once you have lost a dog you loved, can you ever fully give yourself to another dog? I don't know for sure. I would like to think it is possible. Remington was softer in disposition than Smoke, still stubborn, protective in the strong silent type way, still judged the integrity of your deeds over words, tolerated fences but not fools, dynamic in the field, comfortable at home and an easy companion.

And then there was Jack.

JULY 2003
HISTORIC FREDERICK MARYLAND

Jack became another beat in my home in July of 2003. Age eight weeks, on the Friday after the Monday my most recent ex-wife told me I could not have another dog. Remington had died over two years ago, and I needed a dog. I had stopped traveling and was doing whatever it was that I was doing for Flynn McPherson. Time and money were plentiful. I called Jerry, told him I wanted a field trial dog, asked if he could get me a Saighton's dog. Maybe there would be another Blue Ridge Smoke in my life. No, he could not. Talbot had died a couple of years ago at the age of ninety. There would be no more Saighton's. The hand-written inscription in my copy of *Spaniels for Sport* reads "To Bart with Best wishes. Have fun with the Authors, Compliments Talbot R, May 1993."

Jerry gave me Ian Openshaw's phone number, who had bred the 2002 UK National Field Trial Champion Moonbeam Flush to Whitehope Shee, and the puppies were ready to leave home. Yankee dollars found their way to the UK, and Jerry even collected Kilpunt Shallot upon arrival at Kennedy airport. His call name had to be Jack, after Mr. Daniel's whiskey, or Union Jack, or Jack whatever.

Just as comparisons are inevitable, so are regrets. The last time I was at Pondview was to drop Jack off for training. I did not know Jerry was selling the place for some be-squillion dollars and retiring from training. I had been coming there for nearly two decades, and this news was troublesome. Ian Openshaw was visiting from the UK with his wife Wendy. Jack forgot his name and did not make a good first impression. There would be more field trials.

Since then, Jerry has been inducted pre-posthumously into the Bird Dog Hall of Fame. Oh, everybody knew he'd get in, just not while he was still alive. I lost the bet.

NORTH DAKOTA PHEASANTS

Jack suffered a bit of a stroke at age six, leaving the left side of his face a little out of kilter and needing eye drops twice a day. I would not let him ride shotgun with his head out the window anymore. Jack had distinguished himself on the field trial circuit, just not favorably. He was great in training. The stroke and his lack of field trial points did not place him in high demand for breeding.

Mike Wright was the head of the Morrison Knudsen Washington office and lived in Maryland at the time. This provided the opportunity for some memorable fly-fishing trips and bird shooting at Hill Country Hunt Club, which Jack and I joined in a vain attempt to replace some portion of life on the farm. Soon after she earned the distinction of being my most recent ex-wife, and after seventeen years of downtown life, she headed south with a significant portion of the proceeds from the sale of our house. Mike and I were enjoying a libation at The Tasting Room after a shoot at Hill Country.

"I'm going home to see my mother next month. Why don't you come out, bring Jack, and we will hunt wild pheasants?" Mike offered.

Jack and I had not been on a road trip since we went to Grants Camp a couple of years before. "Fantastic idea; I'm all in." Jack had never hunted wild birds. Smoke and Remington had that pleasure in their time. It would now be Jack's chance.

Mike's sister and brother-in-law farm thousands of acres in his native North Dakota, and they are all ours for the better part of a week.

Jack and I load up my Range Rover with everything we think we might need, including his kennel, even though he rides shotgun most of the time. He does not always like staying in hotels, much prefers sleeping alone in the truck, and for his safety I put him in his kennel. He is, by his own wishes, a nothing in, nothing out traveler.

It takes us three days to get to Mike's mother's home in Hazleton. A stay in Minneapolis at a high-rise Residence Inn with an elevator ride to our room on the fifth floor brought forth the same look as the boat experience at Grant's Camp. The gas mileage on the Range Rover had gone down significantly, and I thought it might need servicing. This was another time when the kennel came in handy. If you have a bird dog in the truck, you move to the front of the line.

Mike's brother Greg was there, along with his kids, and his mother took her whiskey neat. There was some talk about Jack sleeping in the house, but after some food and water, he thought the car would be better. The temperature dropped unexpectedly, and he was shaking cold in the morning. We moved the truck into a barn and provided blankets for the rest of our visit.

This is the first time I've ever seen pheasants roosting in a tree; we might be a bit early. Having hunted wild birds on opening day in Nebraska for several years, I thought I knew how: You find a likely looking field, park the truck, set the blockers, let the dogs out, spread out the shooters, and work into the wind. Wrong. I knew the roads would not be paved, just packed-down dirt. What I didn't know was you just drove till you saw some birds along the side, then you hop out and shoot.

The worst possible thing to be is the driver. The guy riding shotgun jumps out even before the truck gets stopped and has already emptied his gun before you can get out from behind the wheel; much less let the dog out. Mike shot a bunch of birds before I figured this whole thing out and kept my gun beside me while driving just to have a fighting chance for even a long shot. There is probably some law prohibiting such. Our limit filled; we decide to check out the nightlife in Bismarck.

Protocol dictates that when you see a game warden parked along the side of the road, you stop and pass the time of day with him. This is especially important when you have out-of-state tags on your truck and it is obvious from your blaze-orange shirt that you are most likely pheasant hunting. So, we stopped, quickly broke my side-by-side, and unloaded before he could get out of his truck and cross the road to inspect our licenses and count how many dead birds were in the truck. Mike introduced himself as one of the Wright boys from Hazleton, and that took the edge off the interview, so all was good.

Being one of the Wright boys from Hazleton worked well another time when we approached a very hostile-looking rancher to ask permission to hunt his land. He thought we were deer hunters from out of state, and somebody had already not only gotten a jump on deer season but shot one of his cows. It took Mike some effort and time, but he had a friend when we left, without hunting, as the rancher had reported the incident to the authorities, and we did not need to get further involved.

We hunted all kinds of terrain, from rolling grassy hills, to harvested grain fields, to swamps with cattails, to overgrown orchards, to abandoned railroad tracks cut into hills and flanked high on both sides with tall grass into the wind, funneling scent of a hundred pheasant's right up Jack's nose. He was way ahead of himself here, flushing everything, out of range, scenting was way too good; flushed an owl over a fresh kill.

Mike was not exactly familiar with hunting with a flushing dog. It took him a bit by surprise that Jack would get airborne after a flushed bird. Luckily, he adapted and only shot the bird. Jack's pads were rubbed raw, so a visit to a vet in Steele was necessary; got all the stuff needed to make them right.

We had limited out three days running. I chose a big beautiful rooster to take to a local taxidermist, who said it would take about a year. It did, and it graces my home with a brass plaque:

Wild North Dakota Pheasant Flushed and Retrieved by Jack, November 2009.

Tomorrow, deer season begins. It's time to leave, but we need one more night in Bismarck, and it is Friday. Mike's cousin owns the N.P. Depot, a Mexican restaurant housed in the historic Northern Pacific train depot. Some folks from the Corps of Engineers with whom Mike has had business dealings, including a brigadier general whose daughter was once Miss North Dakota, join us. The General invites us back to his house for some port and cigars. She was not there. We pick up a couple of bottles of good port, one for the cellar, one to be enjoyed on a beautiful warm evening on the deck overlooking the Big Muddy. There are lots of stars over North Dakota. Some even fell.

We covered a lot of territory, primarily southeast of Bismarck; some of the most beautiful vistas imaginable, unspoiled prairie as far as the eye could see interrupted by the occasional flat-topped mesa jutting tall from the prairie grass. It is two hundred years ago. Roaming herds of bison are grazing in the distance. The light at sundown turns the wide empty prairie into soft prisms and lakes of color. The air glows pale yellow. Lewis and Clark are camped over the next ridge.

It's deer season. Nothing left to do but head to The Orchard. There is no longer a gathering place. There is not even a free-range chicken to be found.

One of us doesn't want to go. The other one rides shotgun.

SEPTEMBER
THE ORCHARD, MARYLAND

Jack was at Brookwood Kennels, no longer in training for field trials he would get to run and retrieve if only a little. I had been at home in The Orchard since returning from a skirmish with the trout of the White River in Arkansas back in May. J.R. Pruitt arranged a trip, which included some good times in Little Rock. A tropical storm a few days before our arrival had made the river almost unfishable; water was flowing over the top of the dam.

Melancholy had set in. I needed to be somewhere other than The Orchard. I don't like to get on airplanes much anymore. It's a "been there done that" way too often to be a fun thing. However, when a friend has a really good idea…

Mike Wright and I arrived late in the day in Last Chance, Idaho. We took the scenic route out of Ashton. Potato fields are flat as a pancake right up to where they run into the backside of the Tetons without so much of a foothill to stop them. They rise straight up, deep purple, against a high blue sky all the way to heaven. The route takes us to Upper Mesa Falls on the famed Henry's Fork of the Snake River. The river plunges one hundred fourteen feet into a cauldron of volcanic rock sending off a cloud of mist that becomes a rainbow as it lifts above the cliff. We are here to fish for rainbow trout on the fly.

Mike had rented a two-bedroom cabin on the property of the Angler's Inn. The only other place in town, just about, is the Trout Inn, and as usual on junkets with Mike, he had an old friend who lives nearby. George and his wife Jackie joined us for dinner our first night at the restaurant in the Trout Inn. They had worked together building some secret government laboratory years earlier. George was inspirational. He is retired. Jackie is much younger and still works at the facility where Mike first met them. Mike is still not retired, and I am nearing the birthday that will be the end of my sixties.

Mike has been here before. A couple of years ago he fished here with his father-in-law Hill Mason. It was on that trip that they met Hootie, who guides out of Mike Lawson's Henry's Fork Anglers. After a long, fun night with George and Jackie, we struggled to meet Hootie for our first day on the water a little too early to be civilized.

We had Hootie for two days. His plan was to float us down the Box Canyon first, and it turned out to be pretty good as we each hooked and landed some very nice fish. Ahead of us, as we floated through the tall narrow cliffs, an Osprey attacked a fish that was too big for it to carry away. We did not catch it either. Mike got the prize for the biggest fish, landing a four-pound whitefish early in the float. It is about an eight-mile trip, putting in at the headwaters below the dam to the top of the Harriman Ranch. We floated past the Angler's Inn where I caught a nice rainbow on our way to take-out at Morrison Bridge.

The Henry's Fork Foundation was formed to restore these fabled waters to their former glory. They have done an admirable job. We had a full day casting grasshopper imitations to, and ultimately catching, big wild rainbows. Dinner was at the Angler's Inn and it was excellent. It was so good that we asked to personally thank the chef for a job well done. We had already gotten to know the bartender. Ann might have been the sous chef, but she joined us for a drink or two and a good time was had by all, pretty much ensuring we would dine again there the next night.

Our second and last day of fishing was another excellent day. We're floating in the Box Canyon was very rough some Class 4 water. Hootie was out of the boat guiding us through the boulders. Today he could just sit and row. We started in the wide-open calm of the ranch, putting in north of Last Chance. The river becomes skinny as we drift The Meadow section of the ranch. There is an oxbow with tall reeds and a flock of half dozen white pelicans lounging on a sandbar. The fishing is productive here. It is a peaceful eighteen-mile drift to as far as you can go without going over Mesa Falls.

Fishing today was again wonderful. I missed three trophy rainbows, landing a couple that needed to grow some more. Could not care less, the scenery was beautiful, and it was not The Orchard. Mike did not miss a beautiful trophy rainbow. The take-out got a little tense as Hootie overshot the ramp. The sound of the roaring falls is much more enjoyable from dry land. He recovered and got us back to town in time for happy hour. By now, we had become well known by the staff at Angler's Inn, some other guests and a few locals.

We began our evening with drinks on the deck looking out over the river soaking up the warmth of the early September sun. Dinner was served as the sun set behind the distant soft purple mountains. Later, we were joined by Ann and some local folks who were there celebrating the twenty-first birthday of our server Gail.

The temperature dropped as we finished dessert and our after-dinner drinks. I photographed her and promised to email her when I got home. She stood a tad over six feet, athletic, and quite pretty. Mike was finishing his wine and settling the tab as Gail took my arm leaving the deck. I threw one arm and half of my jacket around her without fully taking it off. It was very chilly. Our cabin door was not locked, nor was the bedroom door. It did close, but not enough so that when Mike arrived with much bluster and a bit sooner than I had hoped the mood was broken.

There are still three months left to fulfill my goal.

Ph.D. Penelope has not yet returned to England; she is still under thirty.

"Just as aging fisherman and the sagging lover boy can one day only dream of the fabled ones that got away, so too both can later muse with an old man's secret smile over those that didn't," John D. Voelker, 1953.

THE ORCHARD

General Hancock spent his last night in The Orchard at the home of Dr. J.J. Weaver, a prominent civic leader, physician, banker, farmer, historian and noted author. His home was on the north side and had a tall, old white Cumber Water Pump in front of the house alongside the road. There was only one road. It runs for a little over a half mile east to west, known as the National Turnpike. Maple trees line both sides of the road forming a canopy that in autumn is stunning. Twenty years later Dr. Weaver, Jr., having followed in his father's footsteps, purchased the lot across the street and erected the grandest of all the homes in The Orchard, the first in the county to have indoor plumbing.

The home remained in his family until the passing of his granddaughter Grace Estelle Fox in 1985. Miss Grace was a friend of my grandmother and my mother. As a young lad I often tagged along when Miss Grace hosted an afternoon tea. Not because I liked old ladies or tea, but the fear was if left alone, I'd wander off into the fields with my dog Jinx. Something those two ladies found to be unacceptable. A wet muddy dog, worse shoes, and a dead rabbit were not welcomed with open arms. My grandmother was much more interested in teaching the young girls in town how to get a bowl of soup from the stove to the dining table without spilling the soup. Don't look at the bowl, watch where you are going.

I remember the first room on the left as I entered her house was the parlor. The centerpiece was a fireplace with a large curved black marble surround. Off the parlor was the study, where large glass-fronted bookcases lined walls floor to ceiling, filled with books and a doll and toy collection gathered on her travels. A very early version of the Teddy Bear dated from the very early nineteen hundreds. She had a remarkable collection of fancy French dolls that were bequeathed to the Carroll County Historical Society and have disappeared. A beautifully carved secretary filled with writing materials graced one wall. The room held a mystery of faraway places and unfamiliar objects from distant places. The memory still fascinates me.

Miss Grace did not live full-time in The Orchard. Truth be told, she was not born in The Orchard. She was born in Washington, D.C., where she owned a home on S Street NW. To escape the oppressive heat of the Washington swamp she would take up residency for the summer in The Orchard, following a tradition set by her parents. Even then she often traveled the world for months at a time. The stories of her travels are now dim in my memory.

At the time, most all the townsfolk were retired and spent their days on their front porch swing waiting for a car to go by so they could wave to whomever. Travel was on Friday night to Westminster, seven miles. Some folks took pride in not having been out of the county in thirty years. For those who did get out of town, Philadelphia was a favorite destination for visiting relatives and shopping in Wanamaker's Department Store.

A Saturday night catfishing on the Monocacy River would be talked about for months, surpassed only by getting to fish the Potomac. Going to bed with the chickens was a way of life. A lot of the men still young enough to work did so at the cement plant in Union Bridge or the Western Maryland Railroad. Their work was not much to talk about unless somebody lost a finger coupling a railcar or fell into a silo of cement dust and died.

FOX HOLE CLUB

Back then it was my notion that Miss Grace was a missionary. A church-sponsored missionary who traveled to Third World countries to convert the heathens to Christianity. She was not a church missionary. She left a professorship at Sarah Lawrence College to join the U.S. Department of State in 1935 and was appointed Historian for the United Nations Relief and Rehabilitation Administration in 1943. UNRRA, a unit of the State Department, provided humanitarian relief to displaced persons in occupied Europe. It was the forerunner of The Marshall Plan. Alger Hiss was very influential in the Department of State during this time. There is no record of her activities during the eight years prior to joining UNRRA. During the war years she visited the occupied countries and authored scholarly dissertations on civil rights in those countries under Hitler's control.

The UNRRA was not a long-lived organization. Harold Glasser, a deep cover spy for the Soviet Union, was employed there, as were at least four other members of the Communist Party, some spies, some not, maybe. Glasser was a member of the Karl Group, one of several covert Soviet spy groups operating in Washington. He also had connections to Columbia University.

Miss Grace was attractive with long, dark-brown hair, which she wore tied up in a bun. She dressed rather stylishly. Her family had always been wealthy and leaders in their communities. She had been educated in the most elite schools and taught at the very upper crust of east coast colleges and universities. A Vassar B.A. led to a Columbia University, M.A. at about the same time The Frankfort School sought refuge there. She was a scholar, historian, professor, poet, and author. Spending her summers growing up in The Orchard, home to four hundred citizens, then and now, who tend to be southern in speech and disposition, yet patriotic to the Union, did not prepare her for resistance to compassionate communism. A "Fellow Traveler" …

Oxford University invited her as guest lecturer for a summer school session. With the permission of King George VI, she was granted entrance to the tower library of Windsor Castle, where she conducted research for her Columbia doctoral thesis *"British Admirals and Chinese Pirates, 1832-1869"* (1940). This work is 225 pages of pertinent facts of interest to no one. The pertinent facts are verified by about ten thousand footnotes.

The question is why? One theory is that there is a secret code of immense national security importance. Why else would it sell for $200? It was winter; the King granted her a small coal stove for warmth.

She visited the capitols of Europe, Southeast Asia, and Japan, the tropics of Central America, and Mexico, when world traveling was difficult and even dangerous. There is no record of her having a traveling companion. Her mother kept a detailed diary, but she did not. Most of all she was a teacher.

The Orchard became the focus of her teaching later in life. I had found my way to other parts of the world before she organized the Fox Hole Club in the early nineteen-sixties. The membership was open to every kid in town between the ages of five and twelve. The club met every Saturday in the basement of her home and made entrance through the door under the back porch, hence, the Hole. She served fresh lemonade made from real lemons, no sugar, and store-bought cookies. At ten o'clock sharp the Book Mobile would stop in front of her house and the club members were encouraged to check out a book of their own choosing. The requirement was to read the book and then write a report about what they had read. The youngest were encouraged to present a picture report about something they found interesting.

Residents who knew her then labeled her "prudently generous." She often took club members to her home in Washington for lunch and sightseeing, the ballet, or even the circus. She would arrive in The Orchard in late spring accompanied by her dog Bunty, a housekeeper, and sometimes a gentleman friend. There were years she kept a horse in her back lot and would enjoy riding cross-country to distant towns as far away as Silver Run visiting friends. Whittaker Chambers' Pipe Creek Farm was near Silver Run. She may have first met him when they attended Columbia at the same time.

After the McCarthy hearings, during the Truman Administration and carrying over into the Eisenhower years, the government cleaned house of communists. McCarthy took names and published them. The Lavender Scare was in full force. It was a cleansing of the Department of State. They did not publish names. She never married. Her curriculum vita does not provide illumination into her activities after 1950, save a brief teaching assignment at Goucher College in 1953-54. Miss Grace suffered a stroke in 1978 that ended her time in The Orchard. She recuperated in her Washington home and lived but another seven years. She only enjoyed The Orchard's water in the summertime.

SUMMERTIME EARLY-1950s
THE ORCHARD

Franklin Nyman was the freckle-faced, redheaded, second stepson of the Methodist minister. The Cold War was in full bloom. The Farm Bureau was paying farmers to build ponds as a hedge against barn fires. Franklin and I were in the third-grade learning to duck under our desks. He and I did not mow other people's grass, make hay or milk someone else's cows, and we had none of our own. There was little else to do. We spent many summer days catching pan fish, never a bass, in the large ponds on the farm at the south edge of town. His older brother was not into fishing or girls.

The farm specialized in poultry. It had a good-sized herd of Black Angus cattle, pigs, and assorted ducks. A brick manor house rests on top of a knoll overlooking a stream fed by the overflow from the ponds. A summer kitchen and springhouse were close by the house. At the foot of the hill is a bank barn, a corncrib, and a long, low, covered building that serve as holding pens, all downwind. The house was shaded by sycamores and maples that have been there for a hundred years or more.

One fine sunny summer's day Franklin took a notion to catch some brim. He found me in my backyard throwing a baseball off the side of the house. I brought along Jinx.

We were halfway down the farm lane, bait-casting rods in hand, when we noticed something was not as it had been. There were lots of black official looking cars with U.S. Government license plates blocking the lane halfway down the hill, so they could not be seen from the main road. They surrounded the manor house. Two huge men dressed in ill-fitting black suits, bulges under their arms, white shirts, narrow black ties, black gum shoes, turned us away.

Jinx didn't like these guys, became loud and nervous, never bit anyone before, but this was different. His lip was turned up, teeth bared, deep growls mixed with angry barking. This was like he didn't like Clarence Dingle on steroids. This was getting ugly, and all we wanted to do was catch some brim. I took off my belt and made a leash and grabbed Jinx by his collar, pulled him back just as the smaller of the two G-men took a kick at Jinx. He missed. Nobody kicks my dog. He was a bit surprised that he was being called what he was being called and took a step back. I yanked Jinx's leash and turned tail and ran up the hill. Franklin was fifty yards ahead of me. We didn't look back till we reached the main road, no one in sight. A couple of scared kids went home and took the dog with them, never said anything about it until now. Never went back again that summer. The Hiss v Chambers confab was in the news. Chambers' "Pipe Creek Farm" was a few miles to the north.

The next summer we gathered courage, trekked to the pond, left the dog home. Everything was back to normal; still didn't catch a bass. The owner of the farm commuted by car to somewhere every day for his real work. He had joined the Army in 1942 at the age of fifty-two. His registration card indicates he was employed by the War Production Board, Washington, D.C. He held a doctorate in chemistry and had been an executive in the chemical industry in New Jersey. Western Maryland College sold him the farm in 1945. The same year the War Production Board was disbanded. Camp Dietrich was not far away. It was later designated a Fort and became the center of the Army's biochemical warfare research. Chickens and eggs were in high demand.

Jinx would flush a pheasant in the summertime.

MAY 21, 2015
GARDEN TOUR
TEMPERANCE

"I believe in every drop of rain that falls a flower grows." Frankie Laine 1953.

Thank God, it's raining.

We have had little rain since it stopped snowing and besides, I'm tired and need a day out of the garden.

I am still having a difficult time coming to grips with living here, and now I've agreed to open my garden for a fundraising event sponsored by the town. I don't know why. There is not much to do here and there has not been for as long as I can remember. My grandparents bought the house in 1925. They were living in the "Union Meeting House" at the top of the hill and my mother, at the age of thirteen, was thrilled to "move into town."

People who live here live forever unless someone incarcerates them in a nursing home, then their life expectancy will probably not exceed ninety years, otherwise they are looking at triple digits. My mother made it to ninety-seven. It's the water. Maybe it's also gardening, if you garden or if you don't the only other thing to do is drink. Unlike my parents, I manage to combine the two.

WINE AND ROSES

"Wait until next year." Brooklyn Dodgers, 1953

The Garden Tour was Sunday noon to five, it is now Tuesday two days afterward.

Recounting yesterday, I awakened at 3:20 a.m. and talked myself out of bed to watch the Open Championship in the coolness of my kitchen, which I assumed was on ESPN. Wrong, they did not begin the broadcast until 6:00 a.m., noon British Summer Time. So, I went back to sleep on the couch. The long and short of it is I watched most of the Open with a catnap every now and again, which caused me to miss the final three holes of the playoff. Damn, I'm still tired.

The Garden Tour has cost me about 15 pounds and three inches of waistline. I am not going to calculate the dollars and cents contributed to The Orchard Improvement Association that will be determined next April. It was this past April that I started the redesign of the garden. I cannot say for sure if the five cubic yards of black mulch was the major expense, or the ten Bobo Hydrangeas to add a little contrast to a future green hedge of fifteen privets, or maybe the other perennials I felt were necessary, just to add a little color. All will be better next year.

The centerpiece of the garden remained unchanged. Entering from the garden gate, there is a raised bed just before the large old American boxwoods that border the patio and close enough to the ancient dogwood that the eye captures the scene, but the sun does not cast its shadow. The square bed is edged by a low hedge of wintergreen boxwood and contains three Souvenir de La Malmaison roses. They are from the bourbon variety first grown in 1843, the year the house was built, in the gardens of Malmaison that was owned by Napoleon's wife Josephine. They were originally known as "Queen of Beauty and Fragrance." Their name changed when a Grand Duke of Russia took a snippet as a souvenir from the gardens of Malmaison and planted it in the Imperial Garden in St. Petersburg. The roses repeat from early June all the way to November barring a killing frost. They tend to rest in mid-July and did so.

Gardening was a matter of family tradition and maybe pride. I got the last pitchfork of mulch off Ted's red pickup at 11:20 a.m. Sunday. The hedgerow of Knockout Roses appears to be well cared for, but they are not in bloom. It was hazy, hot, and humid. It had to have been over 100 degrees when, after four hours and twenty minutes, I stopped. Showered, dressed, resplendent in a pink linen shirt, dark blue jeans, new white tennis shoes, and my Brooks Brothers seersucker sport coat, which I bought in 1985 and my most recent ex-wife hated. It was way too hot to be resplendent for long.

Kat has rescued me once again, always the perfect hostess, this time she made potent sangria in a big jar with a spicket at the bottom. The party was on the porch. It was over 100 degrees on the patio. Babs brought Jill and Matt, who found himself a chair within arm's length of the spicket and had a wonderful afternoon. Jill turned out to be fascinating and Maureen O'Hara lovely. She lives in downtown Frederick; chances are I will run into her there some time or another. I hope I will remember her and she me. Kat also picked up the cheese tray I ordered from the new shop on 2nd Street, and Solo cups which I did not have time to get. Brought her violin, played several snappy Irish tunes to much praise and pleasure, and looked divine in a long strapless black wrap. Gave me the chance to brag on her about when she played the violin at Carnegie Hall before she was old enough to buy a beer.

Cousin Bonnie and Ted came to collect their red pickup truck and left a half case of beer. I invited Mr. Hyatt who, after reading an early draft of this epistle, was disappointed to learn how little English he taught me in high school. The committee that organized the Garden Tour was put out that I was having a party serving adult beverages. One or two joined us on the porch and did not overstay their welcome. All my guests bought tickets to visit the other gardens on the tour, contributing to the town fund.

FEBRUARY 3, 2017
THE ORCHARD, MARYLAND

The air smells like snow.

It is a curiosity when I find a good guy, and then that guy knows another good guy that I know. It happens though and did again last week at Noontootla Creek Farms.

Hill Mason celebrated his seventy-fifth birthday on January 30, making him fifty-four days younger than me. He has held up much better. His favorite son-in-law, Mike Wright, being one of the most considerate and generous good guys on the planet, arranged a celebratory cast and blast expedition to Blue Ridge, Georgia. Keith, Hill's son, whose home faces Lake Champlain, joined us. It was colder in North Georgia than it was in Vermont. We found comfortable accommodation in Noontootla Creek Farms, Granddad's House. This whole adventure conforms very well to our annual Goose Camp gathering and throws in Trout Camp just for fun.

Noontootla Creek is a small scenic stretch of private water and holds big rainbow and brown trout. All were born wild in the creek. It is catch and release, fly fishing only. Mike and Hill have been here before, about five years ago. Then, as now, and on many other adventures, Mike has hired Hootie as our guide. Hootie is a native of the Blue Ridge, born and bred, known locally as Big John. He guides here in the winter and on Henry's Fork in the summer. He is a character unto himself. He does not wear a toe ring. He is taller and leaner than Mike, a head above me and thirty or so years younger. Has years of uncut red hair, and once in Idaho a broken right hand. I established the toe ring thing six or seven years ago when I was first introduced to him in Last Chance. He has always put us on fish.

Hootie showed up around nine in the morning. He brought along his buddy and fellow guide, Hunter. Hunter is a big boy, tall, wide, and thick. He is from the Blue Ridge mostly, throw in some Cherokee from Bryson City and you got a good ole country boy, pretty much the same as Hootie without the Cherokee and save the red hair.

Hunter is assigned Hill and Keith for the day on Noontootla Creek. Hootie gathers Mike and me up, loads us in his pickup, heads down the road and across the pasture, parks under some trees next to creek side. No reason to walk, it is cold. Hunter, Hill, and Keith head the opposite direction.

There are what look like snow clouds trying to climb over the mountain to the west. The creek is narrow at best. Trees overhang on both banks, knocking down whatever wind there is; Hootie says we are going to take turns casting in the same pool. Mike goes first. Hootie figures, correctly, that Mike will be responsible for his tip. There is a pod of trout hanging around a ledge under an overhang about ten feet straight out from us. Looks to be ten or twelve good size ones sitting quietly waiting for a morsel to drift past. They are not looking up for a meal. There is a bit of a challenge here. To get a nymph to drift into their eating range, the fly must be presented upstream, so it will sink and drift right past their noses. Trout are lazy in the winter.

Mike reasons if he false casts about thirty feet of line downstream, he will be able to then forward cast upstream to the proper spot to allow a good drift. He tried this approach fifty or more times without even a glance from the trout. I studied this exercise from the near bank. Never got the fly close enough to them. On my first cast, I used the same strategy of casting downstream, letting the back-cast travel upstream, except as the line straightened out a flick of the wrist and the tippet took a hard left and landed near the far bank. It caught in the far-left edge of the current and came downstream, threw an upstream mend to slow it down. The third cast was perfect.

A Rainbow trout longer than from my index finger to my elbow was brought to Hootie's net. We moved to a different pool. Mike goes first again. Same story, only this time the trout was bigger. We move again to a different pool. Mike goes first. Same story, the trout was even bigger. This one was a brown. I never did tell him about the wrist flick. We moved to a different pool. Mike lands a good size rainbow trout. Hoots and hollers echo off the side of the mountain. The snow clouds are getting closer.

I did not want to go back to the creek after lunch. Hootie provided some nondescript sandwiches from the local Food Lion. They are included in his fee. I was tired and my back hurt. It is cold and spitting snow. Mike persuaded me — insulted me -- back to the creek. Some bullshit about age. Happy he did, more great fish for Mike and I got a couple as well.

"I knew someday it would come to this," I said as Mike had one arm, Hootie the other, dragging me upstream to another pool. My legs had stopped working. Somehow the humor they found in this escaped me.

NOONTOOTLA CREEK FARMS
BLUE RIDGE, GEORGIA
DAY TWO

Breakfast is cereal and coffee, self-service.

We are to show up at the main farm office at nine o'clock to meet our guides for today's bobwhite hunt. We are on time and decline a round of sporting clays. Upon entering the office my memory is jolted back, I recognized our guide but could not recall his name, walked back outside to check out his truck. Just as I thought, remembered his dog to be a Brittany Spaniel, name is Belle. I was here two years ago with J.R. It was the time J.R. had what I thought was a heart attack. I don't think Carter remembered me and I did not attempt to remind him. It gave me comfort to have recognized him and remember Belle is a good dog, they call her Miss Belle.

The guide introduced himself as Carter Morris. Guides who hunt over good dogs do not sport rings on the middle toe of their left foot. Mike and I will hunt together along with Miss Belle. Hill does not get to spend much time with Keith during a year. This is good family time for them. I told Mike I remembered Belle and she does not hunt close but can find birds.

Carter is my age or so. He had a long career in the Navy. He served most of his years at the White House, said he might be the only guy to make captain without ever commanding a ship. He is still active in the reserves. His stories are good, and I find him a very interesting companion in the field. He found my sixteen-gauge side-by-side much to his liking. His son Hunter is a fishing guide and works on the Soque with my dear friend Glad Simmons. Carter thinks the world of Glad, good people. He thinks the Simmons's might like to adopt Hunter. By lunchtime we had harvested a dozen birds.

Miss Belle needed a break, she must be around five or six years old, now.

Once again, I yielded to Mike's persuasion and returned to the field for more shooting. It turned out to be the right move. We hunted a flat field between two mountain ridges bordered on one side by Noontootla Creek. At one time it had been a crop field, now it was a quail field. Belle came to point at a patch of broom sedge near the trees that lined the bank of the creek. Carter kicked out four quail. They hurtled up out of the broom sedge heading for the trees. I emptied both barrels, a clean double. Mike got another, and one escaped through the trees, over the creek and up the mountainside. Hawks need to eat too.

"Good shooting," came from Carter as he sent Miss Belle after the first of the double. She had a good mark, a straight out and straight back retrieve. Miss Belle was sent after the second bird of the double, Carter had marked it and with a few whistle commands, she brought it to hand. Mike's bird was a total blind retrieve both by Miss Belle and Carter. Mike had a general idea where it fell, and Carter put Miss Belle to work again. It fell near the creek bank and the cover was thorny dense. It took some doin', but she found the dead bird and brought it directly to Carter. A damn good day's work on just three birds.

After the double I could not hit the side of a barn. Took a seat in Carter's truck and watched a while. Mike had a good afternoon. He and Belle chased a covey up the mountain on the far side of the field. The birds escaped into the laurel. I laughed out loud.

BLUE RIDGE, GEORGIA

We are back fishing with Hootie and his friend Hunter Barnes. This time it's a float trip on the Toccoa River. The Toccoa is not a catch and release river. We are thinking of catching supper. It is cold. The river is high and dark. Mike shares a boat with Hootie and Keith. Hill and I load into Hunter's drift boat. I settle in on the forward starboard side. Hill takes a position aft on the port side. This allows us both to be able to cast to either side of the boat without getting our lines crossed.

The fishing is not good. Keith and Mike seem to have had some luck. Hill and I have not. It is snowing. It is cold. We are all ready to head home. We are drifting close to the right bank and I cast toward the middle and upriver some. A brown trout in full color is fooled and becomes the best and last fish of the day. Hunter says his Cherokee grandfather says it is bad ju-ju to kill a brown trout. Hill and I hope the other boat caught some supper.

They had, and Keith grilled them to perfection. This is our last night. There is bourbon before dinner and delicious wine with dinner and as usual Jack Daniels after dinner for Hill and me. The other two stick with wine.

Keith knew our gathering this time of year had become a tradition. This year he would have made the fifth to our foursome, but Ron had once again backed out. He did not know when we first began this tradition. The first time I met Hill was on the Salmon River trip in Pulaski, New York. It was this trip that began the Hill, Mike, and me gathering, from time to time supplemented by others. Ron was on that trip along with Mike and Flynn McPherson.

"Do you guys remember the time we were fishing the Salmon River in Pulaski and Ron claimed to have saved Flynn's life?" I asked.

"I don't remember, was it on the river or in a bar?" Hill asked.

"I think on the river," Mike said, "the day we fished the Donaldson Run. We paid extra to fish there. I think it was the only day we caught fish. We got up early it was still dark as we hiked down to the river wearing miner's lamps on our heads. Sandy Smith, the good guide, arranged it."

"What did Ron do to save his life?"

Nobody remembered.

"Call him up." An idea almost always brought on by an overindulgence in adult beverages.

That's how we found he was in Phoenix about to board a flight to Washington. He didn't really remember either, just claimed Flynn was about to fall and he caught him. Flynn was a robust fellow with a big appetite for life and it is perfectly imaginable that he almost fell. He would have been either hung over or still drunk from the night before. The trip to the Salmon River was the first time we all had fished together. We had not yet become The Campers.

"Who's Flynn?" Keith asked.

"He was an old friend of mine," I said.

Flynn McPherson owned a large conglomerate of various enterprises. Hill was still a Philadelphia lawyer. Mike and I worked for Morrison Knudson, and MK had hired Ron to consult with Mike at my suggestion. Thank you very much.

I had known Flynn for a long time, and we had hunted and fished together many times. Almost always ending up in a strip joint, my left ear is deaf because of him. That's another story or two, maybe even three. I first met him sometime in the early 1980s. I don't recall the exactly how, but I think it had to do with building a new facility for one of his businesses.

"He's dead now, some ten years or more," I said. "There was a time we had a bunch of fun."

Mike asked, as he flicked the ash off the end of his cigar landing where his filleted trout once was, "What year was the Salmon River trip? I don't remember."

"Must have been around 2000, October I believe, cause that stupid shit-ass guide, what's his name, announced at dinner on our last night that he supported Hillary for Senate. I would not have tipped the sumbitch anyway. Damn lucky, I didn't shoot the bastard."

"You didn't like him, Bart?" Keith.

"I need another drink. The son-of-a-bitch was the worst damn guide on the planet, ever. The guy with the toe ring on the middle toe of his left foot out of Jacksonville was bad. J.R. and I fished with him a total of three and a half days and never even saw the first fish, much less catch one. He was a true South Beach dandy, could even say slick. Too slick, not an honest look about him. He could not find fish and we just did not like one another. Earrings are tolerable, toe rings are not. This bozo in Pulaski was the worst."

"He called himself Chip," Mike chimed in. "He put us elbow to elbow in a line with dozens of other guys on a small creek, so small you could practically step across it. Had to use a figure eight roll cast with lots of lead on the line, and he tied on some kind of nymph, don't remember what it was."

"I know what it was not," I said, "there was some guy upstream who kept catching one salmon after another and worked them downstream, making everybody downstream reel-in as he passed by. As he went by the third time, I asked him what fly we were using. He said Montana Green Worm."

"I don't remember what Chip said we were using, but it was not a Montana Green Worm, and when I asked why not he said he didn't think they would be any good. That was as the guy came down the river for the fourth time, just a stupid ass."

"I don't remember exactly which happened first, him grabbing my rod or me throwing it at him. We had moved to a different part of the river, still cheek by jowl, and he kept yelling at me to stop the back cast at twelve o'clock. All we could really do was a role cast; only needed ten feet anyway. The damn river was not that wide, and the leaves were off all the trees along the bank. It was not even a very pretty river. I was standing in the middle, above knee-deep water and hooked my first and only fish, it was a righteous hook-up, and he grabbed the rod out of my hand, waded to the bank and ran off down the river bank and around a bend so we could no longer see him. After a while he came back, "Where's the fish?"

"It broke off."

"Shit man, I could have done that."

"I was still in pretty deep water. He was still bitching about my casting, nobody else, just mine. I was getting pissed off. I was wearing neoprene waders and my green, waxed cotton, three quarter length jacket I had bought at Purdey's in London. It never failed to keep me warm and dry, still have it hanging in the pantry, thirty some years later. I want to be buried in it. It was the only thing in Purdey's I could afford, and I thought I had money then. Right now, I have no idea what he said, but cussing him with obscene ferocity I threw my rod at him, hit him in the head. He headed to the riverbank rubbing the left side of his face and I reached down into the deep very cold water to retrieve my rod from the bottom of the river. My arm did not get wet."

"I saw him do it," Mike said, "Thought there was going to be a fight, but he kept on going, don't think we saw Chip again until the next day." Cigar smoke necessitated the opening of the kitchen windows.

"Is there more port?" I asked. "Never mind I'll switch back to whiskey."

I continued the story, "That night some of us ended up with Flynn in a strip joint, some of us did not. The next day Flynn did not show up for breakfast. He did find us on the river, about ten o'clock. It was snowing, and he had a short sleeve shirt on, no coat or hat. I don't think he knew where he was. This was very typical behavior when Flynn was out of town. He was the epitome of decorum when not."

Hill and Mike could not remember if Flynn fished at all that day. He disappeared while trying to find a hat and coat. Flynn claimed, later, that he went back to meet one of the strippers from the night before, had her name and phone number. This too was very typical when he was out of town. There is no evidence that happened. Being the great humanitarian that he thought he was, Flynn contributed mightily to the scholarship fund of many a pole dancer.

Chip was dull, even stupid, and a complete ass, but he realized he needed help because I had threatened to go shopping for a gun. The next day he brought along Sandy Smith. He was good. Mike and Hill used him a couple of summers later on Cape Cod for stripers. In Maryland, we call them rockfish.

That night at dinner in a very cool place with a view of Lake Ontario, Flynn bored us near to tears with the drama involved in the impending sale of the largest of his holdings, which was also a division of another holding. To oversimplify, the drama resulted from the fact that Flynn owned forty-nine percent. He wanted to end up owning the smaller cash cow outright. The selling price was a hundred thousand short of a billion. The cash cow was not worth very much in and of itself, relatively speaking.

The long and short of it, as it happened some months later, was that Flynn got his forty-nine percent, bought the cash cow for damn little, and a couple of farms for tax purposes.

One of the first things Flynn did after taking control of the cash cow was to hire J.R. Pruitt in June of 2001, upon my recommendation. Flynn would have hired him anyway, but he did ask, and I did say do it. I did not work for the cash cow exactly. It is rather unclear what I did there and should remain so. However, I was handsomely rewarded for whatever it was I was doing. Flynn would have been considered well-to-do even before he became really rich. As a one percenter, and now being the top dog, our trips became more frequent and to great places, and his scholarship funding became even more generous.

"Was the Salmon River trip before or after the time you guys were out in western Maryland?" Hill asked.

"Yes, I'll have another drink, thank you. That trip was before the North Branch of the Potomac trip. That's the trip when Ron, suddenly and without audible explosion, engulfed the entire bar room in a putrid flammable gaseous blue haze that caused a human stampede out of the bar. The bar at the Red Run Lodge became unfit for human occupancy. I was standing way too close to him, singed the hairs in my nose, my eyebrows smoked, eyes cried, it was Biblical." Laughing hysterically, tears on my cheek.

"It was God-awful," Mike said laughing. "Could not breathe, stumbled outside, there was a mad rush for the door, must have been twenty folks headed for the patio all at once."

"Sorry I missed it," sarcasm from Hill.

"Yea, you should be," Mike said. "Ron was buying."

"That's hard to believe."

We didn't know where Flynn was.

"We had met that morning at Eaglehead Golf Club in Mt. Airy. We played nine holes, and it was on the par three seventh that Ron yanked an eight iron out-of-bounds on the left, 'take a mulligan.' He did, and it went in.

"He was still jumping around, up and down, proclaiming his joy at the top of his voice, could have been ten years old, as I entered a three on the scorecard.

"Mike reminded us that tradition holds a hole in one requires the lucky golfer to buy at the nineteenth hole. In our case, the nineteenth was in the Red Run Lodge. And the lucky bastard had caught all the fish in the afternoon on the Youghiogheny River. If anyone had tried to light a cigarette, the place would have exploded."

There is a hotel by the bridge that crosses Deep Creek Lake. We could each get our own room, and it had a German restaurant attached and a bar with a band. The restaurant was celebrating Oktoberfest. The bar was standing room only, jam-packed with local talent, one such was a blond and one a brunette, both were very cute and about thirty years too young. My mustache had not yet turned gray. After dancing with each, alternating for some time, the brunette became a little too drunk, slurring her words. The blond volunteered she had been checked for HIV and more last week and was clean of everything. The brunette was drunk. I had worn myself out.

"Good night guys, see you at breakfast."

That next day, Flynn must have suspected something, as he had drawn up a fifth chair at the breakfast table. I was late in arriving. The others had already ordered their bacon and eggs, potatoes, no grits. There was fresh coffee on the table.

"Will she be joining us?" Flynn asked.

"Who?"

"You know who," snickering.

"Do I have time to eat before we get up with the guides?" I poured my first cup of black coffee.

"We'll wait, you probably need the energy."

We were late meeting the guides. They took it in stride as Flynn and I had fished with them last year, and I suspect they did not expect us to be on time.

We were to fish the North Branch of the Potomac that day.

The river was down. The day was warm. A light breeze delivered the sweet smell of autumn. The water reflected the yellow and red fall foliage as it wound its way through beautiful canyons of the Appalachians. It was barely knee deep and the slow flow was gin clear. We put-in at the Kitzmiller ramp and waded down river from the West Virginia side. The conditions seemed to be perfect. The fish must have thought so too, and chose to enjoy their day without being tempted to eat a fly of any kind. After a bit, the guides said they did not really want any more of our money and called it a half day. They joined us for a burger and a beer.

Last year at the same put-in ramp Flynn and I crossed to the West Virginia side in a thigh high flow without the need for a wading staff. Hiked up-river on the railroad tracks to find Love Pool and had a full day of catching rainbows and browns. On the way back across the river that afternoon the water had come up, and we were tired and thirsty. Hank, our guide, was holding Flynn by an arm leading him across in what was now chest high water and much too fast for anyone to be wading. There were no other fisherman on the river, it had become unfishable. I was wading behind them relying on a stick we had picked up along the riverbank as a third leg. It was old and a bit rotten. The damn thing broke about twenty yards from the Maryland side. It threw me off balance and the current was dragging me under. I looked down river, trying to spot a rock that I might be able to grab hold of as Hank caught me by my left arm just as my waders began to take on water. He pretty much dragged me to a slower current where I could get my feet under me again. Then arm in arm to dry land. Flynn was safe on the bank. I bought Hank a beer or two.

Keith had gone to bed long before Hank saved my life. Hill was nodding off and Mike wanted me to tell the Goldschlager story. I went to bed.

JULY 30, 2017
THE ORCHARD, MARYLAND
THE BELLS HAVE NAMES

It feels like a beautiful Carolina late-September morning, except it's The Orchard and it is late July. A gully washer of a storm blew through here yesterday and cleaned out the dreadful mugginess, leaving a pure blue sky. In the distance a church bell calls parishioner to services; I recognize it as "Little Becky," the bell that for one hundred and twenty-five years graced the steeple of St. Paul's Lutheran Church. My grandmother, the daughter of George Washington Baughman, Pastor of St. Paul's at the turn of the twentieth century, told me the bell was donated to the church by Miss Rebecca Mehring and bears a plaque to that effect. She told me the names of all the other church bells, but I have forgotten them. She wanted "Little Becky" to chime once for every year she was old when she died, that would have been one hundred and two. It is the water.

I did not remember in time to make that happen.

She also did not want the hearse carrying her coffin to pass by our house for fear her spirit would not want to go where it was going, preferring to stay earth bound. I did remember that; suggested it and was summarily rebuked. There are some that believe her fear was well founded and the hearse should have taken the long way around.

"Little Becky" now welcomes a St. Mark's Orthodox Syrian congregation. Two years ago, they removed the Syrian from the church sign. The Lutherans did not propagate well. The demise of St. Paul's cannot be laid at the feet of G. W. Baughman. He inspired three young men from the parish to take up the Lord's mission, including his son Harry F. Baughman, who later served as President of Gettysburg Theological Seminary for many years.

Later, after eggs and oven-baked bacon, another, closer bell peals, signaling ten o'clock services. There are two churches remaining after the Great Fire of 1976. The Church of God and the adjoining parsonage burned to the ground. The steeple collapsed and the bell tumbling, crashing, ringing its death knell, still sends shivers down the spine. My house was next door to the church. The rafters in the attic are charred, but it stands otherwise unscathed. A young rabbit stopped by my breakfast table for a moment on his morning journey, unhurried. It had been in the herb garden, nibbling weeds.

James Galway is playing Mozart's Concerto for flute and harp softly in the background. The coffee is black and strong. A wren sings from the dogwood tree shading the patio from the morning sun. A pair of red-tailed hawks circle overhead glistening in the sun, shirking at each other, the overstocked flock of English Sparrows has taken shelter. It is an otherwise quiet Sunday morning.

The catbirds showed themselves early before coffee. They have become stealthy in their movements and quite of voice. One paused in the dogwood tree, surveying the landscape before quickly flitting onto its nest in the variegated holly tree. It has an insect in its beak. It makes the meowing sound from which their name derives as it feeds the young in the nest. The meow is fussing "this is the best bug you will get today, eat."

They arrive here in late spring and have for the past ten years. Their spring song is a pleasant lyrical tune. They go to a quiet meow when their young hatch. This year they started to build in the boxwoods as they have the past nine years. A cardinal was building in the holly tree. They ran him off and moved into that tree farther removed from the patio and my breakfast table.

Someone within earshot has cranked up a motorized yard tool. A choir of other such devices as the day progresses will join it. This peaceful Sunday morning has come to an end.

JULY 2017
THE ORCHARD

Before motorized yard implements, such work was not done on Sunday. The summer evenings must have been longer then. There were vegetable gardens to be plowed, cultivated by hand, planted by hand, fertilized by hand, insecticide applied by hand, weeded by hand, and harvested by hand into wicker baskets. Chickens needed to be fed by hand, eggs gathered by hand. Those who had a cow milked her by hand. Sam King took whiskey while slopping his pigs by hand. His wife Rosie did Grace Fox's laundry by hand. A steady hand sheared burrier Cookson's sheep. Wilbur Devilbiss & Sons Trucking picked up the trash every Saturday. Wilbur drove the truck; Fisher loaded the trash by hand and for free. Everyone's grass was mowed with reel-type mowers pushed by hand. All was done quietly.

Sunday mornings were for church. Sunday afternoons were for fried chicken, iced tea, conversation, and visiting. Early Sunday evenings were for a drive in the country to escape the chimes that blared forth hymns from the Church of God steeple. Loudspeakers broadcast the Lord's music to the countryside from seventy-eight rpm records. Five miles away was a pleasant distance to enjoy the music. Thirty feet on Wednesday and Sunday evenings was hard to endure. There are no more chickens, vegetable gardens, outhouses, or barns, and the chimes went down with the church. There's only grass that needs to be cut three days a week and always on Sunday.

The noise agitation faded into a quiet, peaceful Sunday afternoon with wine and Stephanie. Conversation was easy, being the lone patron at her bar in the Red Horse. It is now past sundown; I am back on the patio, reclined in the hundred-year-old white wicker rocker. There is still a glow in the western sky. The motorized yard grooming has stopped. Drifting in and out of a wine sleep; there was a presence at my feet, the young rabbit, nibbling.

Saturday mornings in the fall were for gathering leaves with a leaf rake. The fallen maple leaves that formed a spectacular canopy of color throughout the town were raked into small piles in front of the house. There was fifteen feet of gravel between the brick sidewalks and the paved road, more than enough to allow car parking in front of each house and several piles of raked leaves. On windless Saturdays the piles would be set afire. The spicy acrid smell of burning leaves will always bring back memories. As the fires burned out and the smoke cleared, neighbors would gather in small groups to share the past weeks happenings while awaiting Walter Renzler with his butcher wagon. A converted pick-up truck with a chopping block for a bed and wood paneled sides with meat hooks holding sausage, beefsteaks, lamb chops, slabs of bacon, and sweet breads. All fresh cut on the chopping block bed, all without refrigeration or even a fly strip, and all the best ever.

Most of the brick sidewalks are now concrete. There is less than three feet from the sidewalks to the paved road. The sidewalks did not become wider. There is now a double yellow line down the middle of the road. There is no longer a need for a leaf rake. The maple tree canopy is now gone. His son-in-law, Mr. Myers, eventually replaced Mr. Renzel. There has not been a butcher wagon in fifty years or more.

Mr. Myers' son Elwood ended up becoming the owner of a supermarket in Union Bridge, specializing in custom-cut meats. Before Elwood left The Orchard, I remember racing him down the street, him driving a red tractor pulling a wagon full of hay and me on my first two-wheel bicycle, which Peter Baughman taught me to ride on Seminary Ridge. The red two-wheel bicycle was left in the dust. A big smile, the wave of a hand, salutes a skinny kid.

1950s
THE ORCHARD

Elwood "Country" Myers took up boxing while still in high school training at the YMCA in Westminster.

The armistice in Panmunjom was hardly a week old; the YMCA boxing team was engaged with a Marine Boxing team from Quantico. "Country" was the reigning Maryland and South Atlantic YMCA heavyweight champion. His second-round knockout of his Marine opponent caught the attention of a major, and the next day Elwood became a Marine. I was in the fifth grade and still riding the red two-wheel bike on the street without a double yellow line down the middle.

Christmas that year brought a new fancy red two-wheel Roadmaster bike, with an enclosed double top tube with a button that activated a horn when pushed. It was geared to go as fast as I could peddle.

Jinx and I were still roaming the hills and woodlands back of town. World War II had ended eight years ago, the cession of fighting in Korea helped Wimpy get out of the ammunition box building business, and he setup a barber shop at the east end of town. A weekly visit was necessary to maintain a proper flattop haircut; fifty-cents included a straight razor trim around the ears and back of the neck. It was best to get there early in the morning. Wimpey was subject to having a nip or two or more; sometimes it was wise to forego the razor trim. There was a pool table. It became a place to gather on Saturdays and keep up on the news of Elwood's career. Elwood's successes inspired Junie Flickinger to take up boxing, also at the YMCA. Junie's career was short-lived, a broken nose his reward. He quit high school, joined the army, served two years, returned to The Orchard with a new red 1958 Chevy Impala convertible, and took me and Hattie to a local corn field. He kept a souvenir pillow from Natural Bridge, Virginia on the back seat.

He drove that same 1958 Chevy Impala to New York City after Christmas of that year. I was not allowed to go; forced to listen to the greatest NFL game ever played on the radio.

Wimpey's ammunition box business was staffed by German prisoners of war. Someone flipped a lit cigarette into a pile of sawdust. The ensuing fire was extinguished by the Germans, saving the first manufacturing business in The Orchard since 1890, when the Union Tannery closed. There were still three churches. The Church of God had not yet burned down, St. Paul's was still a Lutheran church, and there was the Methodist Church next to Grace Fox's house. The Nyman's had relocated to Edgewater, still in Maryland. There were three stores, Furmalt's on the east end sold dry goods, penny candy and Flying A gasoline. The one at the foot of Lazy Hill, across the road from the Union Meeting House, sold AAMCO gasoline and had the air raid siren mounted on a pole. Devilbiss's store housed the post office and sold everything else including the best homemade ice cream in the world.

Slowly but surely the stores closed. The Flying A went first. No one was moving out of town and no one was moving in, there were no houses for sale and there was nowhere to build a new one. It was necessary for a death to occur to buy a house; no one was dying, of natural causes. It's the water. The Orchard had become stagnate, over ripe. It became important to know your family tree. There was incest on the east end of town. It was back off the road and stayed dark. There were still only four hundred residents and no occupying troops.

My years passed slowly and quietly, interrupted by the unpleasantness of little league baseball for the New Windsor Cubs. Elwood's boxing career was progressing nicely. "Country" was now the Marine Corp's heavyweight champion and had qualified for the 1956 Olympic Trials. He won the Southwest Olympic Regional Tournament. It was in Yankee Stadium, September 20, 1955, Rocky Marciano v. Archie Moore, Elwood was on the undercard. He lost by split decision to the guy who lost a split decision to Pete Rademacher, who won by TKO over the Russian Lev Murkin to win the Olympic Championship in Melbourne. The Orchard had another hero.

Wimpey was finishing up Bus Smelser's weekly trim; I was racking another game of pool having lost the last one. Bus was the manager of the Libertytown Little League team. I was playing for the New Windsor team and the Cubs were very, very good. In those days there was no mercy clause. The Cubs would regularly score 20 or more runs a game. We had just beaten Liberty something like 33 to 9. Bus wanted to know why we had to score so much. I responded that we didn't set out to score 33 runs, it just happened. Nobody wants to make an out.

The 1954 Cubs were the first integrated team in Maryland and were undefeated that year, 22-0. They were disqualified from the state tournament...apartheid. I was in the third base line box seats when Frank Robinson hit the only ball ever out of Memorial Stadium in Baltimore, 545 feet out over the left field light stanchion. Mickey Mantle hit one out of Griffith Stadium in Washington the day Franklin Nyman and I were watching from the right field bleachers, 560 feet I believe. My favorite and perhaps the most impressive was off the bat of Sonny Brooks at the Union Bridge Little League field. Cleared the left-field fence and sailed over the roof of the second house up the street. It was not measurable; no one could determine exactly where it landed. He was twelve.

People from The Orchard could call Charles H. Smelser "Bus." Bus was born in The Orchard. He graduated from the University of Maryland in 1942 and joined the United States Army Air Force as a pilot. He flew 35 bombing missions from England in B-17s and was awarded the Distinguished Flying Cross and the Air Medal with 5 Oak Leaf clusters. He was a true Renaissance man, farmer, state senator, banker, and all-around good man.

Clarence Lockard lived right across the street. He had charged up San Juan Hill and signed up again for the Great War. Got shot up at Argonne, kept a diary while hospitalized in France. Returned to The Orchard, started a flooring business, smoked Camels, retired long after I moved on. His daughter still lives there. She is five or six years my elder. It is the water. The Orchard has another hero.

After the Olympics, Elwood retired from the Marine Corps and boxing, Pete Radamacher turned pro and lost his first fight to Floyd Patterson. Many years later my friend John Smith, who grew up in hobo jungles riding the rails, and I were the only two white folks in the Washington Coliseum the night Muhammad Ali beat the b-Jesus out of Floyd Patterson. It was on big screen, and we exited the premises promptly after the fight.

SEPTEMBER 5, 2017
THE ORCHARD, MARYLAND

Fall is in the air.

The old double guns propped in the corner hutch, swabbed, conjuring up images of the dogs they shot over and the game brought to hand. The Benelli Super Black Eagle was cleaned this morning in case someone calls and invites me to take advantage of the early goose season. I have already committed to Still Point Pond in late January.

The last I heard from J.R. there is the threat of a cast and blast trip to the Louisiana bayous for redfish and ducks. The plan being, like last year, I will already be in Georgia after Christmas, house sitting his daughter's plantation and her dog Jake. Jake is a wonderful old dog, part lab and part something else. He sleeps most of the day and all night. He does not like fireworks or thunder. Last year around New Year's a tornado touched down on Gillionville Road about a tenth of a mile from the couch where Jake was trying to sleep. Jake is too old to be as scared as he was. I joined him on his couch.

SEPTEMBER 11, 2017
THE ORCHARD, MARYLAND

I have been here since the middle of January, maybe a little crazy. I had turned my television off for the summer, had it turned back on last week for college football. This morning I found myself standing at attention, hand over heart, shoulders back, gut sucked in, taps and tears. It just seemed to mean more this year than other years.

The storm that blew through here a month ago brought forth the best August weather in living history. Mother Nature forgot August in the Mid-Atlantic is all about heat and humidity. She gave us September a month early. The fruit of the old dogwood turned red this weekend. I have not seen the young rabbit in a month, not a rose in the garden. The catbirds are still here.

About a year ago now Mike called saying he and Hill were spending the weekend at Le Canard and the Striper fishing should be good and could I join them. I was halfway there before he hung up his phone.

SEPTEMBER 2016
LE CANARD

Le Canard is perched atop a hill overlooking the Corratoman River near the confluence of the Rappahannock as it flows into the Chesapeake Bay. There are two Redhead Ducks mounted on the wall next to the stone fireplace and his boat is named the Blue Duck. Mike is from North Dakota, but he has adapted nicely to the land of pleasant living. There is an ample supply of good whiskey, steaks, good wine, cigars, and lies about who shot the Redheads.

We were on the water early Saturday morning cruising the East Branch. Hill and Mike forsake the traditional art of fishing with a fly and cast with spinning rod and reel. The other person on board the Blue Duck is stubborn and stays with a fly rod casting an assortment of yellow flies with no luck. I tried switching to pink and drug a tree off the bottom but no fish.

After lunch in town we were back on the Blue Duck, just past the Route 3 Bridge, near Stingray Point. It was here in 1603 Captain John Smith was fishing and hooked into a Cownose Stingray. Capt. John Smith and I now have something in common, almost. The one I hooked was not really hooked. I had foul-hooked onto someone else's line. The poor beast was thoroughly entangled and put up on fierce fight. As I got her alongside the boat Mike cut away my line. She was panicked, flapping her wings, and thrashing her very dangerous tail. Mike was in a good degree of peril trying to cut away the fouled lines. He came close to being stung by her tail and wished her good luck. Capt. Smith was not as lucky. He was severely stung. His life was in danger. We don't know if it was Pocahontas, but it was a Native American that paddled the canoe across the Rappahannock and up the creek and dug the mud and carried it back across the Rappahannock to where Capt. Smith lay dying and applied the mud to Smith's wound that saved his life. The mud creek shows on navigation charts as Antitoxin Creek, north of Stingray Point.

There were no fish caught of any consequence. The Stingray provided all the excitement we needed for this day. I had tied on a Clouser Blue Minnow and was reeling in my last cast of the day; just as it got close to the boat something hit it so hard it snapped the leader instantly. The next time it will be a Blue Minnow on a wire leader.

AUGUST 9, 2010
LAKE NERKA, WOOD-TIKCHIK STATE PARK
ALASKA

J.R. and I left our gear stacked on the dock and returned to the yurt for hot coffee. It was raining, not like splash-down hard, more like the air just turned wet. The seaplane was an hour late and getting later. The waters of Lake Nerka were gray. The air was gray and wet; visibility was about as far as my elbow. There was no horizon. Apprehension was thicker than the pea soup fog. Time was dragging. I sank deep into an overstuffed more than slightly worn leather chair, heavy white coffee mug in hand and closed my eyes. The wood stove took the damp chill out of the room. It smelled the way wood stoves are supposed to, cozy and homey. We were not going to get to Dillingham anytime soon. J.R. was pacing, nervous and agitated about missing his homebound flight out of Anchorage. I didn't really care. I had planned to stay the night in Anchorage anyway if we got there. Time is what I've got the most of, and I'm in no hurry to get to someplace I don't want to be. It had been gray, cold, and raining on and off for the past week. One day we saw some mountains. The fishing was good.

A couple of nights ago we were roused out of our tent at midnight with the promise of an Aurora Borealis display. There were s'mores by the bonfire on the lakeshore, but no northern lights. It was missing a good chance to rain. David Taylor, the camp owner, was nearer to my age than to that of his young and beautiful wife, who flew in from Hawaii. Bobby, one of the guides, had his young and beautiful Kiwi girlfriend flown in from Juneau. There were no other women in camp, only six crusty old fly fishermen, a couple of scruffy guides, and an old camp cook. It reminded me of the lesson we learned on our first Alaska trip; if you want or need something bring it with you. On that trip the camp cook was a woman. She made chocolate chip cookies for breakfast; just for me, no one else. She could not cook a lick.

Scott D Free was our guide for most of the week expressed much consternation over my very nice Willis & Geiger rain slicker. I bought it used on ebay in 1986 and it has seen heavy use since then. Mr. D Free, who does not wear a toe ring, was fearful it would scare the fish away. It is red. This is its second trip to Alaska.

Scotty knew all the secret spots, the red jacket is credited for attracting one Arctic Char after another, each one bigger than the last and not another boat in sight. Scotty was in his late twenties and had been guiding summers in Alaska for several years. In real life he was a junior high school teacher in the South Bronx, New York City. The ever-present threat of grizzly bears was like a holiday from danger for him. I think the one day we did not fish with him was the day David Taylor decided we needed to take a road trip. We had caught nothing but big, fat, Arctic Char for three days, and a change of scenery was welcomed.

There are no roads. There is a chain of lakes connected by narrow rivers and a day trip to the fifth lake, Lake Kulik promised unspoiled wilderness. The weather could easily turn this into a two-day trip. Scotty got the day off and we jumped into Bobby's jet boat because he was young and strong and a former army ranger with a Purple Heart from Iran.

The trip takes long enough that we need to stop for fuel both going and coming. There we found an impressive glacier flowing off the side of a mountain, with a large ice cave big enough to walk into without bending over. J.R. could not entice me to explore the cave, it is after all August. Bobby gathered some driftwood, rubbed two sticks together, and fixed a hot meal. The fifth lake was very remote and not easily accessible. The fish here may not have ever seen a fly or fly fisher-folk.

After lunch we explored the river that connected us to Lake Kulik from Lake Beverly. I don't know if it has a name or not. We were in a deep green canyon where waterfalls cascaded ten stories down from the canyon's rim and splashed its way into the small river. We dragged the jet boat onto a narrow sand bar with bear tracks at the water's edge. He tied a dry fly on my 5# line that resembled a mosquito. The small stream of fast water emptied into a long narrow clear pool and smoothed out reflecting the green canyon walls. I cast the mosquito fly into the fast water and let it dead drift into the quiet pool as it slowed down in the drift a citation Grayling struck hard. He gracefully leaped, and tail danced across the entire narrow pool before finding his way to the landing net. I did not submit the application. David Taylor estimated it was around ten years old. Grayling in these waters can migrate over 100 miles in a year from their winter homes to summer breeding waters. He was truly a gorgeous creature; large silver green dorsal fin is spotted with red and purple. His silver-gray body has a hint of a blue hue and three pink strips on his pelvic fin. The "sailfish" of the North is a trophy for the ages. He will live to be fooled again by some other lucky fly fisherfolk.

Our camp mates were a friendly group, some had been coming here for five or six years and told wonderful stories of fabulous fish being brought to the net. We did not make any lasting acquaintances except Scotty and David Taylor. We did not make any on the 2007 trip either.

The grayling was the remembrance for this trip. On our previous trip we caught nine different species including grayling. The one here was special. Then we were fishing out of Aniak River Lodge, way north and west of here. Close enough to Nome where people can go for a good time. We did not go to Nome.

J.R. and I had joined a group of eight that was being hosted by Larry Schoenborn. Larry was a television fly-fishing "how to" personality from the West Coast. After a couple of days, he began calling J.R. over to provide advice when coaching his group. J.R. had landed a thirty-five-pound King Salmon. No one else had come close and did not come close the rest of the week. I caught the largest rainbow on a mouse pattern, north of twenty-six inches. The guides said we were still a month away from big rainbows.

The Aniak River Lodge is perched on a bluff overlooking the Kuskokwim River. It is comfortable if not star rated. Aniak is located on an island and there is no economy and no liquor as it is a reservation. Everything costs twice as much as it should anywhere else. We arrive on a 15-passenger Frontier Airlines, propeller-driven, wing flapping, prayer-inducing Beechcraft. Our fly rods were spared the thrill of this flight; mine arrived on the next plane the next day. J.R.'s did not. His went to a group north of us on the Salmon River. A bush pilot went out of his way to drop them off in Aniak. No charge. We could now go fishing.

We had a meet and greet diner that first evening, one group leaving, our group moving in. It is always J.R.'s job to bring the Jack Daniels. He brought one bottle, not knowing we could not buy any locally. One bottle for one week, and we found this out after we had already had two drinks before the meet and greet. Sam Sudore, the camp owner, was the perfect host and offered to have some flown in, everyone was cordial. The next day, our first day on the water, was with Josh and his jet boat.

On his first cast of a Mr. Pink, J.R. caught his first king salmon ever. I needed to hold my jaw differently before I caught my first. Josh asked if we would like to try for some "northerns," we replied in the affirmative. We boated up to the very end of Dead End Slough, tied on poppers, against Josh's advice. The slough was long, narrow, and shallow. The popper worked across the surface of the brackish water, pop, pop, and pop; we saw the pike coming thirty feet away. Bam, an explosion of dynamitic energy, one of the hardest hits I've ever seen, all thirty-six inches of him out of the water. After a worthy fight J.R. netted several pounds of raw energy. A well-seasoned toothpick successfully adjusted my jaw, mine was bigger.

That night at dinner it was just us and Larry's congregation of six teetotalers and a nice guy from Connecticut. J. R.'s arms and mine were tired from reeling in fish all day. We still were able to bend an elbow for one good drink before dinner. Before dinner was served, we were all sitting around the table and I was spinning some yarns about something funny that had J.R. as the brunt. The story could have been about the time on the Deschutes J.R. got swamped and damn near drowned. Or the time in London when I picked up the girl from Minnesota at the bar in the Ruben's Hotel and he trailed around after me like a little lost puppy. I don't remember which it was. Before I got to the punch line the head elder of the teetotalers aggressively, loudly, and rudely interrupted me. "I've listened to you now for twelve hours and you are either a lawyer or a preacher." He did not mean that as a compliment.

"I am neither, but I've been both." That is half true. From that moment on, only Larry and the guy from Connecticut spoke to us for the rest of the week. In fact, we were the last to arrive at the remote camp; four miles up the Aniak we found our tent pitched a hundred yards from the main camp. This made both J.R. and me a little nervous. This is grizzly bear country, and J.R. and I have already had our camp raided once by bears in West Virginia. They drank the Miller Lite, left the Bud alone. If we had been sober, we would have been scared.

We were late getting there because when we reported to our jet boat that morning there was none. The guide we had been assigned quit during the night left camp and took his jet boat with him. Josh, after carrying the teetotalers to the camp, came back and gathered us up a couple of hours later. J.R. and I passed the time on a sand bar catching fifteen-pound chum salmon one after the other. They become a nuisance as the week passed. It takes twenty minutes to land one and that's twenty minutes we could be catching Dolly Varden, Rainbow Trout, Shee "tarpon of the north," or any other variety of salmon. Wild musk oxen were grazing on a distant hill across the river.

The Dolly Varden was the most beautiful fish we caught all week. Locals call them the clown fish. J.R.'s was a large male over twenty-four inches. His light gray body was streaked with red from his head to his dorsal fin and red from its large hooked mouth along the belly to a bright red fin edged in white. Pale spots decorated his back to his tail much like those of Arctic char, to which he is related by evolution. There were many memorable and gallant fish caught and released that week.

Twenty-four-plus inch Tiger Rainbow on a mouse pattern, got me out of the boat, drug me into a strand of timber. Climbing over fallen trees, ducking under others, keep a tight line and the fish out of the bushes, don't stumble and fall, finally Whitey got him in the net, and released. Good God that was fun. J.R. captured the struggle on video, as he did with the twenty-five-pound King I fought to the net with my five-weight on a sand bar with fresh bear sign. Jeff Wasler, knee deep in the river, was handling the landing net with a .375 Ruger slung over his shoulder. He said that had to be some kind of record for a five weight. The next morning, after chocolate chip cookies, I foul-hooked a small salmon in the river by the camp. The commotion caught the attention of Annie, the camp golden retriever; she splashed into the water and retrieved the fouled fish.

Jet boats are fast and not quiet. They would not be the first choice for a wildlife watching expedition. We did get close enough to a female grizzly for a good photograph. I missed one that was too fast running across the river in front of us. We saw bald eagles along the banks of the Aniak, on Lake Nerka and all along the trip to the fifth lake but no bears.

David Taylor's two-way radio was quiet. It was resting on the yurt's fly-tying bench, oblivious to the stares of the anxious travelers. J.R.'s agitation had not improved; in frustration he brushed some loose hackle off its speaker. The radio crackled to life as if it had been waiting for the hackle to be dusted away. The heavy white coffee mug was still in my hand. Our bush pilot was on his way and would be here in twenty minutes. There was a break in the weather that would last long enough to get us to Dillingham in time to catch the last flight to Anchorage. How the pilot found our camp in that weather is a mystery to me. J.R. and I hustled out to the dock, we heard him splash down the de Havilland Beaver long before we saw him emerge from the fog. He did not apologize for the delay. This was serious business; hurry-up we don't have a big window to get out of here. J.R.'s connecting flight in Anchorage had already taken off before we left the lake. He found himself in an ugly and expensive discussion with Delta to get on any flight to anywhere the next day and looking for a hotel room. Having shared a tent for the past six nights I was not about to share mine, and besides, I had other plans.

The bush pilot loaded our gear onto his plane in the fog, balancing the weight. Visibility had improved so that I could now see my feet. He taxied out onto the open water of Lake Nerka, opened the throttle wide and lifted off the water, climbed into the gray clouds, passed over Aleknagik and found his way safely to Dillingham. Arriving there we learned that earlier in the day a de Havilland Otter turbo took off from Lake Nerka heading for a sporting lodge on the Nushagak River had gone missing. The plane was carrying former Senator Ted Stevens and eight others.

Next day, his body was found in the wreckage on the side of a mountain.

SUMMER 2017
A FEW MILES SOUTH OF THE ORCHARD

Flintlock and I were sittin' and sippin' the best corn whiskey ever, reminiscing over Alaska. Not sure where he gets it, made from heritage corn, and keeps a stash is his basement. Flintlock and I had played little league baseball together and knew one another before that and some since. He took to firearms, and I stayed with my long bow, that was a long time ago. He evolved to primitive, and I came to shotguns and fly rods way too late in life, always had a bird dog except for now.

Today he was trying to convince me to hunt deer with a muzzle loader. He has a spare. It was longer than I am tall and weighed enough that it wobbled from my shoulder. Flintlock does not hunt from a tree — he stalks. He has killed more than his share of deer, elk, moose, caribou, and red stag all over the world; every species of turkey known to man, and some that weren't, all with a muzzle loader. He completed the Turkey World Triple Crown in the jungles of south Mexico with a rare Ocellated that nobody ever heard of much less hunted.

He will not set foot on the Dark Continent. Says there are no bears there.

Flintlock is a big man, and no longer a spring chicken. Not that long ago he trekked off to Russia decked out in Daniel Boone buckskins and a John Wayne hat, survived the night streets of Moscow and the train to Siberia, brought back a trophy Russian brown bear. He knows all about the species of, and the sub-species of, every bear on the planet, and has killed everyone with a muzzle-loading flintlock, except the great white one.

I decline the deer invite. There is no dog involved. He retrieves more of the best corn whiskey ever, sipping straight from the Mason jar. Laments he can no longer drive a nail with his long rifle. Doesn't hear worth a damn either, and neither do I

Says Alaska's the only place he has been he could not walk out of, well, and maybe Russia too. He is a survivalist. I am not sure anyone could walk out of the south Mexican jungle, but what do I know. I think ruffing it is a Hilton Garden Inn without a bar. On a previous trip to the Kodiak Region he killed a brown bear as big as a Volkswagen. Looming over the two of us is the grizzly he shot in the Arctic tundra, upright on its hind legs. It is bigger than the one in the Anchorage Airport.

I had just finished relating my Lake Nerka, Wood-Tikchik State Park, Ted Stevens story, a little more dramatically than necessary.

Flintlock started, "Well now Skitter," he said with a touch of competitive drama. "I was way north of where you were, forty-five miles north of Anaktuvuk Pass and seventy-five miles from the Arctic Ocean, it was day six of a planned ten-day hunt. I figured this to be my last bear hunt. This one was important. We had spotted and turned down several juvenile bears. I was here for a trophy, not yet worried, but a bit anxious. I was carrying this." He handed me the beautiful .54 caliber long rifle made to 1790 roundball specs, made by a Maryland gun maker special for him. I almost dropped it, gave it back.

"Also, had on my hip, as a backup, a .58 caliber flintlock pistol made before 1805 by Phillip Creamer. He was a Maryland gun maker from Taneytown. I like to keep things local."

"It was cold and cloudy. I was tired. Five nights in a tent at my age took a toll. My guide was glassing a thicket of alders on a small mountain. He spotted what seems a rock at five hundred yards just short of the alders and hands me the binoculars."

"The rock moves, it is a silver-tipped grizzly." Excited now.

The stalk begins; "Skitter," his voice softer now, full of apprehensive, "I knew this was the one and maybe the only one we would get a chance at. The wind was a cross breeze. The bear would not get our sent. We had to cross a knee-deep river, deeper in some places, full of Grayling, I worried about falling and keeping the powder dry. It took some time."

"Once across the river we stopped, glassed the hill again, the bear has moved, disappeared. My heart was in my throat. Where could he have gone? This guy was why I was here, we must find him."

The great bear became aware of intruders into his kingdom. The stalk ends. The hunt begins, again.

"The guide said he has a mark on the spot where we first saw him. I can breathe again."

"Several hours passed; nothing, finally we found the spot where the bear had been bed down, sign and tracks were plenty. I needed to sit down, gather myself, drink some water. It was getting late in the day, we had forgotten about lunch, but there was still plenty of light. After a couple of false trails, we find one that held some promise, fresh sign. He was not far away. More water. We moved slowly down the trail, my heart rate was in the red zone, could the bear hear it pounding? Despite the cold, sweat poured down my face, take another drink, pulled a red bandana from my vest and tied it around my head Apache style. The wind had shifted, it is now at our back."

The bear too is searching, curious, defensive, protective of his territory.

The intruders keep looking, still glassing the mossy tussock of stump tundra looking for anything that moves unnaturally.

"A ptarmigan flushes from a patch of alders off to our right. We crouch down to keep our profile below the scrub bushes. I know he can hear my heart pounding."

"Suddenly, there he was close and downwind right in front of us." Flintlock's voice pitched higher, excited, animated, off the couch now raised the rifle to his shoulder.

"The bear had caught our scent, stood up on his hind legs."

"The long rifle jumped to my cheek. It was still primed, from the first stalk and I hoped dry, double-checked. I figured the ball would drop about eight inches in the one hundred -forty yards. I cocked the hammer." Still living the moment.

Exhale deep, squeeze softly, a puff of white smoke, a round ball is sent into the great beast's chest. The grizzly flipped backward spinning, biting, and clawing at the wound. He circled twice, saw the white smoke, and came charging, head down mouth open. Flintlock can reload in twenty-three seconds.

"I blew down the barrel to clean out the sparks."

The bear was charging full speed. Flintlock does not have twenty-three seconds.

"I dropped the gun with the ramrod still in the barrel and fumbled for the pistol. The guide raised his .300 Winchester. My hands were shaking bad and wet from sweat, before I could cock the pistol hammer the bear stumbled— and piled up dead." Less than twenty steps from two sets of white knuckles. "I collapsed on my knees, exhausted, relieved, grateful and humbled."

My Mason jar is empty. "Flintlock my friend, you are a brave man, maybe a little crazy. I don't think I would've lived through that, but I do have one more trip to Alaska in me."

I must remember to bring everything I might need or want with me. I may or may not bring a fly rod or a private stash of whiskey. I will bring `whatever else I think I might need or want and leave enough time to allow for having a good time and missing flights. I need to rethink the fly rod.

It is the best corn whiskey ever.

DECEMBER 23, 2017
CHRISTMAS ROAD TRIP

Louisiana redfish and ducks did not happen, and I doubt it ever will. I guess I don't care much. Panama City Beach is good enough for me. This year I got to J.R.'s house on Christmas Eve, three days before I was invited. Stopped by Orangeburg on the way, it is still a two-day drive. Did not go to the Chestnut, drank dinner with Junior and Betty Lou. M.T. was with her nanny. Junior asked if I'd ever eaten something that sounded low country; I said no I hadn't. He cooked up some of whatever it was I hadn't eaten before and I think it's safe to say I still haven't.

J.R. booked both Blue brothers for two days of duck hunting on the West Bay. Both days turned into half days of hunting in the afternoon. The morning fog did not lift. One afternoon I shared a boat with Bill and one brother and the next with Franz and the other brother. Conversation was slight, as was the shooting. J.R. was in the other boat, anchored a few yards away, hidden largely by the dense fog. He tried to relieve the boredom with some humorous, off-color tales that reflected poorly on my love life. He asked me at least twenty times to tell the Goldschlager story. The Goldschlager story is best told when consuming prodigious amounts of alcohol, which we were not. Bill is much too serious, and Franz had heard them all before.

For two days there were thousands of ducks a half-mile from where we set out the decoys and they stayed there, and we stayed where we were and remained quietly bored. On the last day, in the last hour, an unfortunate pair of Hooded Mergansers came out of the fog directly over my boat. By the time I saw them and stood up it was a fifty-yard shot. That is why God made Benelli's and 3½" shells. There was some talk that next year we would give up on ducks and go for quail. The sun finally set, ending the day without another shot being fired. I needed a change of scenery.

Jackie answered her phone. I asked her if she'd keep me company, if she'd drive, I'd buy. We had a fabulous evening with dinner at the Grand Marlin. The next morning J.R. and Franz went home and took the drake Hooded Merganser I shot during the afternoon hunt with them. It was the only duck shot either day. He now graces my kitchen wall. I stayed an extra day. Jackie invited me to dinner at a seafood spot on the west side of town. There was live music, her mom and dad, aunts, uncles, old family friends, and former babysitters. The music was good, the food was better, and photos of me with a dead duck helped break the age-difference ice.

The next day I found my way back to Albany in time to assume my dog sitting New Year's duties with Jake. The weather cooperated, no tornados, and Jake and I had an uneventful four days together. We took long morning walks and shorter afternoon walks, staying on the paths through the woods. When he wore out he'd head toward the back door of the house. One afternoon he tried to run some; managed a few quick steps. Other than the walks he spent his day on the couch. A cushion has been removed to make it easier for him to climb up.

Jake slid off his couch, came into the bedroom and stood quietly at the door watching as I packed my stuff. He had never done this before. He followed along behind as I carried my luggage to the kitchen door. As I opened the door, he stopped. I put my bag down, his eyes were sad, his tail slowly wagged, I gave him an affectionate ear rub. We both knew it would be the last one.

It is good to love and to be loved.

MARCH 18, 2018
POULENC AND THE PINES
HOOD COLLEGE, MARYLAND

The Pines of Rome, a poem for orchestra in four parts by Respighi, was first performed in 1924, and never more glorious than today at Coffman Chapel. Attending a symphony orchestra performance has never been high on my list of things to do on a warm Sunday afternoon in early spring. There is probably a hatch on the creek. This performance by the Frederick Symphony Orchestra is special. There is no place on earth I would rather be.

"Blackjack" Pershing's own The United States Army Herald Trumpets marched with precision to the front of the altar. "Left Face," the drummer tapped cadence on his sticks, "Present Arms," trumpets brought to lips. Lieutenant Colonel Shaw raised the baton high over his head, with a flourish he brought it down and fourteen unmuffled trumpets brought the audience to their feet. People who could not easily stand up did — with a hand over their heart.

I put on sunglasses to obscure tears of pride. This was not going to be a quiet Sunday afternoon. The energy level was established and continued with Rimsky-Korsakov's *Procession of the Nobles*. More trumpets, a French horn, tuba, trombone, organ, timpani, and percussion, it was a natural loud. A large majority the folks in attendance are Medicare recipients and needed to lower their heart rates. The music obliged with Francis Poulenc's *Organ Concerto in G Minor* conducted by Andrew Rosenfeld. A beautiful concerto with various tempo changes allows the heart rate to moderate before Intermission. Intermission was way too long, but it allowed Ted to visit with his old friend Andy Rosenfeld. I found some old Second Street neighbors and caught up on the last twelve years.

The Herald Trumpets returned and raised the collective heart rate with a short medley of military marches. They were a proper prelude to the centerpiece of today's performance of Respighi's *The Pines of Rome*. We were told to be alert for the "singing birds" at the end of the third movement. They would introduce the final movement *The Pines of the Appian Way*. It celebrates the triumphant return of the Roman army with all its spoils and splendor. Ted said he first heard this work when he was in high school, I don't think I've ever heard it and certainly not as it was performed today. The Herald Trumpets had slipped unnoticed down both sides of the Chapel. The birds sang. The trumpets blared, the organ's pipes were in full throttle, the strings vibrated, the windows rattled, the building trembled it was loud beyond comprehension. A standing ovation with hoots, hollers, foot stomping and hand clapping applause may have been louder.

Think I'll quiet down on the creek, pretty sure there will be an evening hatch.

I can fish Friends Creek anytime but have not since December with Kat. It was our annual Christmas outing, early this year. The creek was frozen solid, a perfect excuse not to pull on boots and waders, not that we needed one. The lobster bisque complete with large lobster tails was perfect. There was an ample supply of wine, none of the best corn whiskey ever and no cigars. So, it was not perfect. Our walk to the end of the property was beautiful and uneventful and littered with fallen trees. I am having a time coming to the realization that it is now more difficult to do the things that I once did ten years ago or even five years ago. Well, even last year. Back in the Nutshell, more wine, Kat announces she has a new boyfriend. The reason I have not met him is he travels a lot for his job. I am skeptical there must be something I would not like about him. "Not so," she assures me, "he has honest eyes." Another glass of wine and, "Oh, by the way, I auditioned for the Frederick Symphony Orchestra and my debut will be in March second chair violin."

The Orchard's catbirds returned to the garden early this year.

-30-

About the Author

H.B. West began his forty-year career in the Construction Industry as a business development executive in New York City. Representing major international engineering/construction companies afforded him many opportunities to explore the world. As retirement approached, he once again fell in love with the pleasures of his youth, bird dogs, fly rods, shot guns and lovely ladies.

CPSIA information can be obtained
at www.ICGtesting.com
Printed in the USA
BVHW030923101121
621186BV00008B/509